I dedicate this book to my beautiful wife, Mary Ellen, without whose love, support, and encouragement this would not have been possible. She also served as a sounding board for all my ideas and first drafts and provided new ideas of her own.

And, of course, to Keke, that lovable imp who danced her way into our lives and made herself right at home in our hearts.

I0571427

Acknowledgments

As the saying goes, "It takes a village." Although I come from a writing family and have been writing throughout my life, I only seriously took up the craft in the past few years and only thought of writing a book in the past several months.

I owe a huge debt of gratitude to Millard Johnson's two critique groups, Writers of the Villages and Writers of the Villages South, who taught me so much about writing. I have also gained much knowledge through my membership in the Writer's League of the Villages and the Florida Writers Association.

I received encouragement from numerous friends, family, dog owners, and fellow writers from two other writing groups: Pen, Paper and Pals; and Wine and Words. I am also grateful to my faithful followers on Medium and Substack, who read my blogs every week and showed their love through their likes, claps, and helpful comments.

It was the love and support from all these wonderful people that gave me the confidence to start on this book.

Finally, a big thank you to my beta readers, Rick and Kim Rozelle, Anne Waters, and Susan Jordan, all of whom gave me extensive feedback that helped me perfect my manuscript.

The Dog Park Massacre

A collection of fun and heartwarming stories
from

Keke's Guide to Training Your Human

Keke

and Ken Van Camp

Credits

Cover design by Mehreen Shaukat.

Lesson 1: photo by Josephine Martin
Lesson 6: photo from Microsoft Office stock
Lesson 9: photo created by author using PhotoCartoon
Lesson 25: photo Creative Commons by Andrea Di Falco via Wikimedia, picture of Keke added by author
Lesson 26: photo by PublicDomainPictures from Pixabay
Lesson 27: photo by Amanda Henderson
Lesson 39: photo of Zoey by Amanda Henderson; photo of bat by Jose Miguel Guardeño from Pixabay
Lesson 40: photo by Autumn Mott Rodeheaver on Unsplash
Lesson 42: photo by Delaney Van on Unsplash
Lesson 43: photo of Keke growling orders by Renata Gusciora
Lesson 44: photo of pug in blanket by Matthew Henry on Unsplash
Lesson 46: photo by Max Bender on Unsplash
Lesson 47: Outdoor manger photo by Mágson Alves on Unsplash

The following photos were created by the author using DALL-E3 A.I.: Lesson 7, 16, 28, 30, 38, 39 (Biewer Sherlock Holmes photo), 40 (football photo), 41 (Biewer Terrier dancing), 45 (soccer photo), 47 (mouse and cat)

All other photos by Mary Ellen Van Camp

Table of Contents

Forward

Did you ever read Anna Sewell's 19th century book *Black Beauty*, which was "translated from the equine"? For some months, I've been following Ken Van Camp's blog, a translation from the canine by his Biewer Terrier entitled "Keke's Guide to Training Your Human." For the most part, it is a delightful read with much humour, though a serious note can creep in when Keke laments the wastefulness and untidiness of people throwing rubbish on the ground instead of waste receptacles. In an ideal world, "pretty privilege" should not exist, but from her photos, Keke is a cute and appealing little dog. I heartily recommend reading this guide.

    Patricia O'Neill

Introduction From That Meddlesome Human

In early 2023, it had been nearly a year since the passing of our beloved Shih-Tzu, Oreo, and we decided we were ready to love another dog. After several months of searching (and getting scammed), in June, my wife and I adopted an energetic, strong-willed, precocious Biewer Terrier puppy whom we named 'Keke.'

We immediately started sharing pictures of Keke with our Facebook friends and attaching our thoughts about what she might be thinking. As our posts grew in popularity, a friend suggested turning it into a blog.

In July, I decided to try my friend's suggestion. *Keke's Guide to Training Your Human* was born and published on Substack and Medium. A month later, I added a podcast of the same name (sourced from the same material).

I published Keke's blog as a series of "lessons" written from Keke's perspective with two audiences. First, Keke would teach other dogs how to adapt to a new life of living with humans. And second, it would teach life lessons to dog-loving humans. To quote my catchphrase:

How do you handle a Biewer Terrier puppy? More importantly, how does she handle you?

The blog grew in popularity, so by the end of 2023, Keke had over 500 followers. At the time of this writing, Keke and I continue to publish new blog posts every week, and her follower list continues to grow.

The lessons in this guide combine light-hearted stories originating from Keke's actions mixed with a healthy dose of fiction and humor. A few are more serious as I attempt to show growth in Keke's personality, but I always try to leave readers with a smile.

Some of the inspiration for *Keke's Guide* came from my favorite cartoon, *Calvin and Hobbes.* Like Calvin, Keke has a wicked side that occasionally irritates her humans (although not nearly as wicked—or irritating—as Calvin).

Several months after starting the blog, I decided Keke needed some recurring friends to bounce ideas off, so like Hobbes, Keke got a fictitious playmate named *Mousey Tongue* (*Mousey* for short). Later, to support more conflict and create more growth opportunities, I gave Keke and Mousey a nemesis in the form of a cat named *Zoey.* Her character is based on my son's real-life cat of the same name.

Although many of Keke's real-life acquaintances make guest appearances in her stories, Keke, Mousey, and Zoey are the only animals that ever talk.

Also like Calvin, Keke in these stories is destined to remain at a single age forever. Although some stories describe her "becoming" a dog, she will always be a puppy in Keke's Guide.

From the beginning, I pledged to keep *Keke's Guide* family-friendly. Although increasingly challenging to find, I have always tried to avoid stories, movies, and television with heavy use of profanity. Call me old-fashioned, but I think there are better ways to get the point across. In Keke's blog, podcast, book, and audiobook, I never include anything worse than the word 'butt' (and even that used sparingly).

While the vocabulary is at the reading level of an adult, I have met several children who enjoyed listening to the podcast and had no trouble understanding the storyline. The audio version of this book may be fun for them.

Keke's Guide is family-friendly entertainment for dog lovers of all ages. I hope you enjoy reading or listening to it as much as I have enjoyed writing and recording it.

Ken Van Camp

Lesson 1: What is a Biewer Terrier?

The top three questions Keke is asked

Hi! My name is Keke, and I'm a Biewer Terrier puppy. I'm also the author, editor, and potentate of *Keke's*

Guide to Training Your Human, my blog, podcast, and now a book. (And soon to be an audiobook.)

I know what you're thinking. This pup's a pretty big deal! How many dogs do you know that have a blog, podcast, and book about them?

But this book is not about me. It's about you! Yes, you, my faithful canine readers, who want nothing more than to be better human-owners. So sit back on your haunches and read (or listen to) 47 lessons that will help you teach your human the essentials of living in a dog's home.

In this lesson, I'll answer some questions I've received from my legions of loyal fans, which will tell you a little more about me.

Okay, so I lied. I AM a big deal, and this book IS about me. But don't you want to know more about me? Who wouldn't?

So, in reverse order, here are the top three questions I hear.

What is a Biewer Terrier?

If you don't know the answer, you're not alone. My humans never heard of us either until they visited my breeder. Then, I ensured they never *stopped* hearing about us. You'll thank me too someday.

The Biewer (pronounced "BEE-ver") began in the 1980s through the selective breeding of Yorkshire Terriers ("Yorkies"). The breed was initially called the "Biewer Yorkshire a' la Pom Pon," which literally means "I'm a French poodle with a froufrou haircut."

Then came the historic Biewer Rebellion. The breeders were doggedly pursued and forced to change the name.

The American Kennel Club (AKC) coronated the Biewer Terrier in 2021, so word is just getting around. Several of my breed appeared in the Westminster Dog Show for the first time in 2023, all with froufrou haircuts. See my photo at the start of this lesson—a much better look for us, eh?

So, how do we differ from Yorkshire Terriers?

Coloring is the first thing people notice: Whereas Yorkies are black and tan, Biewer Terriers are tri-colored, adding white to the mix. My coat is primarily black-and-white, with tan highlights around my ears and face. I've seen other Biewers with blacker bodies and browner faces, but they are obviously not as pretty as I am. (Sorry, girls, I call it like it is.)

Left unclipped, a Biewer Terrier has long, silky hair, but my mane resembles a chopped, home-groomed puppy clip right now. As a result, I have wild hair like a hedgehog—a perennial case of "bedhead."

Because Yorkie tails are usually "docked", they appear to have shorter, stockier bodies. My tail and sleek physique give me a longer, thinner look. The word *lithesome* springs to mind. My mind, anyway. You may not be a proper dog connoisseur. You might even be one of those poodle lovers. It's okay—you probably never met a Biewer Terrier.

Because the Biewer Terrier's tail is left long, the wagging gives us a friendlier reputation. And did I mention that sleek, *lithesome* look? But we make reputations the old-fashioned way: "We EARN them."

Speaking of friendliness, Yorkshire Terriers are known to be feisty and tenacious. After all, they were bred to catch rats long before they became British royal lap dogs.

Are Biewers feisty? You bet we are! If you have any doubt, see my lesson <u>Getting the Best Treats</u> later in this book. But Biewer Terriers are playful and family-friendly—the life of the party. The crème de la crème. Not a lap dog, although we appreciate a full-bodied cushion at nap time.

Speaking of which, I'm told I have two speeds: High and Off. I like to play hard—my favorite game is a cross between soccer and rugby, with a dash of Calvinball thrown in to keep 'em guessing. I have the spirit of a wild Mustang until I collapse and sleep with all the energy of a sloth having a bad day.

Biewer Terriers are also loving, playful, intelligent, and occasionally spiteful. Which helps make this book even more enjoyable!

Are Biewer Terriers smart?

The second most frequently asked question is about how smart we are. One human recently asked me, "Keke, my dog can barely tell his chew toy from his foot, and here you are writing a blog and a book and producing a podcast! How do you do it?"

Well, I'll tell you, some mornings it isn't easy. I drag my lazy human out of bed to get my coffee and fire up the laptop before I start work. I'm a slow typist, but this is where my dancing skills come in. I can do the Foxtrot, the Carolina Shag, and the Control-Alt-Delete.

I'm the fastest puppy typist in the West. And the East. See the lesson, Keke's Fitness Routine, to learn more about how I type.

The most frequently asked question

And the most common question I get (drum roll please) is, "How did you get so darn CUTE?" If I'm being totally honest, it's a combination of good genes, good haircuts, and hard work at runway model training school. No botox; this puppy is *au naturel*. And did I mention *lithesome*?

To learn more about Biewer Terriers, read more of this book. For the latest posts, follow my blog, *Keke's Guide to Training Your Human*, available on Medium or Substack. Or listen to my PAWDcast of the same name. You can hear it on any of the popular podcast apps or sung by the Vienna Boy's Choir.

Why does the world need a book written by a Biewer Terrier? Because dogs are people too, you know!

Lesson 2: Get them to wear tassels!

Tug toys can be found everywhere

Because EVERYTHING is a tug toy!

Lesson 3: That Pitiful Puppy Look

Even you can show those sad, puppy eyes

Okay, pups, listen up! This is an important lesson, one we'll refer to many times in future lessons, so you may want to poopmark it.

Now, I must come clean here and admit that not every puppy was born with the same inalienable rights. I mean, there's cute, and then there's CUTE. Some of us got it in spades, and some got a few low-value clubs. But no matter what The Good Dog gave you, own it. Work it, baby. You, too, can learn to show those sad puppy eyes even if you're a ten-year-old Chihuahua.

It's best to practice while sitting or lying down, as it makes you look more sorrowful and subservient. It's helpful if you sit or lie down directly on your human's path to ensure they see you and have to take extra steps to avoid stepping on you. (If they do step on you, play it for all it's worth: a prolonged, soulful howl, like a Bassett Hound doing Aretha Franklin.)

Now, lower your ears and relax your haunches, let your upper eyelids droop a little, and close your mouth so your teeth don't show. If lying down, let your chin flow into the floor, and look up. Don't overdo it, or you'll look like you're falling asleep, just enough to show them how sorry you are.

Don't worry if you're not really sorry! You might be thinking of sinking your teeth into your human's privates and pulling them up over his head (we'll cover that in a future lesson). But for now, we're focusing on that doleful, pitiful expression. If it doesn't work the first time, keep practicing and pay attention to reactions. If your human is so worried that they're talking about a trip to the vet, you probably overdid it—but you're on the right track! Just perk up and try again next time. It's never too soon to start training your human in empathy. Or maybe get an extra treat, which isn't too bad either, is it?

Lesson 4: Everything, Everywhere, All At Once

Keep all your toys accessible

It's essential to have all your toys easily accessible wherever and whenever you need them. If your house has a family room, kitchen, or other place where the humans gather between meals, this is the ideal place to keep your toys—in the middle of the floor, of course, so they're ready whenever someone wants to play with you.

Your human may insist on putting them away periodically. "Clean up," they like to call it. I call it a training opportunity.

If they put your toys away in a place you can reach, wait until the human leaves the room, retrieve them all, and spread them out again. It can be a fun game for all.

Sometimes, your human may tire of this game and put your toys away where you can't get them. If this happens, sit in the room where you want them and bark—a slow, monotonous bark, say once every ten seconds. Not often enough to be mistaken for a burglar or fire alarm, but an annoyance that will make them have to investigate.

Sometimes, they will mistake this bark for your "I have to go outside" signal. You can quickly clear up the confusion by returning to the family room as soon as you return inside and repeating your earlier barking exercise.

Humans are not the sharpest tooth in the mouth, but eventually, they'll realize that you want a toy and they'll get one for you.

Play with the toy for a while. Include your human so they feel rewarded and you reinforce their positive behavior. This is how to "train your human."

Once the human leaves the room or gets distracted, hide the toy where they won't find it. Repeat the prior steps until you get every toy back. Then, bring them from your hiding space and spread them across the floor.

Eventually, your human will tire of putting toys away. Congratulations! You have a well-trained human.

Lesson 5: The Importance of Chew Toys

When you're not near the chew toy you love, improvise!

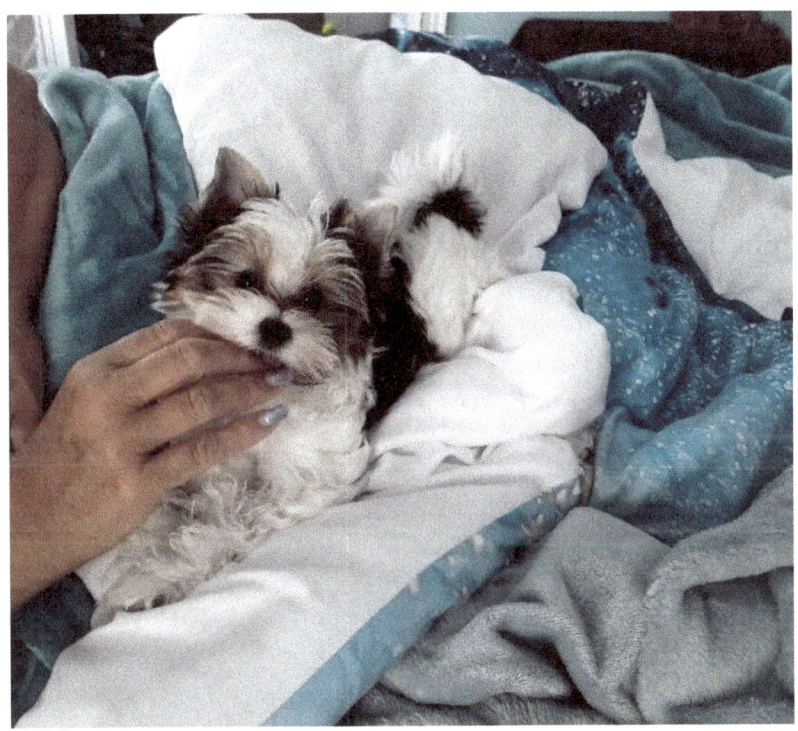

For puppies growing new teeth, "chew toys" are more than a game; they are a salve for the teething process. But for dogs of any age, they can bring comfort, relieve stress, weaponize your relationship with your human, and provide sustenance. You need them when Nike sneakers, hard-brimmed Boston Red Sox caps, James Patterson novels, and smelly jock straps are not available. They are also an essential lesson in persistence.

If you start by chewing on your human's fingers, after the first few "ouch" responses and occasional stitches at the local clinic, they will begin to recognize the importance of buying you things to chew that do not include human appendages. Beyond toys, these may include "chew sticks" such as rawhide or beef jerky. The smellier, the better, I say.

If your human is too cheap to buy what you want, do not despair. Eschew their miserly gift and find something else to masticate. See the opening paragraph of this lesson for a few suggestions, but your options are limitless! As I mentioned in Everything, Everywhere, All at Once, humans learn through positive reinforcement. Once they figure out what you like to chew, as long as it isn't an $800 Giorgio Armani, there's a good chance they'll buy it for you. Persistence is the key.

Lesson 6: Rover's Limerick

Rover's lament

There once was an old human named Grover,

Whose dog-walking days were long over.

He smiled so smug

Till he peed on the rug—

Why didn't he ask to go out, Rover?

Lesson 7: First Impressions Count

No poodles in the house

The other day, my human looked at me and roared, "No poodles in the house!" I thought yep, no argument here. Poodles are a mangy breed if you ask me. They're stuck-up yappers and not all that bright. But I have never been mistaken for a poodle in all my weeks of living.

So, you can imagine my confusion when he looked at me and repeated it. I checked to see if someone had snuck into the house while we talked, but we were alone.

Naturally, I wanted to voice my support for this new mandate. And that's when the idea hit me like the recoil from Kim Kardashian's Spanx. I've heard about the importance of first impressions, so I thought, what better time to try one? Sitting straight on my haunches, I let out the loudest, most annoying yap I could muster. It was rather funny if you ask me—sounded almost like a poodle.

Unfortunately, my human didn't share the enthusiasm for my poodle impression. After disparaging the piddle I left him, he proceeded to chase me around the house until he fell, panting, into the laundry pile.

Maybe I overdid the French accent.

But whoever said first impressions count was probably right. I'll take more time to practice before I try my second one.

Lesson 8: Overcoming Unfair Human Advantages

Distract him!

I was playing "Chase the Mouse" with my human yesterday. The mouse is on a string, the string is on a stick, and the stick is in his hand. A little flick of the stick sends the mouse screaming across the carpet with me in hot pursuit. Instead of arguing over his unfair advantage, I distract him by chewing on his shoelaces. The mouse is back in my mouth in no time.

It's like taking candy from a baby. Yum.

Lesson 9: Dragontooth, Queen of the Unmowed Jungle

Keke finds her inner superhero

In every puppy's life, there comes a day when she must face her fears and spread her paws—a day when a puppy becomes a dog.

The day began simply enough for me: chewing on a table leg, jumping on furniture, and playing soccer with the puppy behind the mirror. That is until I noticed two things. The first was a series of squeaks, and the second was the awareness that the house had no other sounds.

I put my nose in the air, but instead of my humans, I smelled a rat. And not the nice kind like Remy in Ratatouille. Something evil and revolting.

My ears perked up when I heard the squeak again. I looked up and saw a mouse perched on a jar on the table by the couch. I knew that jar: it held puppy cookies, and the lid was off. The mouse had two claws in the jar and nearly had a treat in its dirty grasp.

I looked at the mouse, and the mouse looked at me. He grinned.

How could this be? A mouse putting its filthy paws on my silky delights? The audacity of such a rodent was impossible to conceive. And yet, there he was.

Someone needed to teach this mouse a lesson in manners, but who? It was me or nobody. I surveyed my options. My humans had placed stairs in front of the couch for me to climb from floor to couch and back.

Unfortunately, these were the Scary Stairs. They tried to show me how to use them, but I had yet to climb more than one of the four steps. Narrow and tall, they were too much for a little puppy to master. And I didn't even want to think about the view from the top.

"Hey, rodent," I barked. "Get away from those cookies; they're mine!"

"Who's gonna make me?" squealed the mouse.

"I am," I growled.

And with that, the mouse uttered a series of short squeaks that could only be a laugh. Or maybe a cackle—he sounded like the Wicked Witch. When he finally stopped, he said, "You can't even get to the couch without a human picking you up!"

And you know what? He was right. If I wanted that little rodent, I'd need help. But who? No one was in the house except a scared puppy and a psychopathic mouse.

And that's when I remembered Mommy giving me a nickname recently when I bit too hard on her fingers.

"Ouch," she said. "You have the teeth of a dragon! I will call you *Dragontooth, Queen of the Un-mowed Jungle!*"

Standing at the foot of the staircase, I knew this was a job for a superhero. Sitting up straight and squaring my shoulders, I said aloud, "This is a job for *Dragontooth, Queen of the Un-mowed Jungle!*" I looked down and saw I was wearing a pink shirt with a gold "D" emblazoned on the front.

A burst of energy shot through me as I put my front paws on the first step, then pushed off with my back ones. As my rear feet hit the first step, my front paws reached for the next. I was doing it: climbing the stairs to the couch without help!

As all four paws hit the couch, I turned to my furry intruder, a mouse whose front claws now held one of my cookies. Seeing me so close, he let out the loudest squeal I had ever heard, dropped the treat, and jumped down. I was nearly upon him when he reached the couch, but I overshot and sent the jar of cookies crashing to the floor.

The mouse scurried down the side of the couch, leaving me peering from the top of the stairs. Looking down, I realized how high I was. I was terrified.

The mouse looked at me from the floor and squealed with laughter. "Little Dragontooth isn't so brave when she has to come back down the stairs!"

Baring my superhero fangs, I released a mighty woof and put two paws on the first step. Fearless, I lowered my back feet, then advanced my front ones. Faster than a toy poodle chasing its tail, I descended the stairs and bounded toward the mouse. Boy, was he surprised!

Yelling "Catty-cornered!" I pounced and grabbed him by the tail.

"Let me go," the mouse wailed. Looking at my razor-sharp dragon teeth, he cried, "Please don't eat me!"

After securing the tail with my paw, I laughed, watching the squirmin' vermin. "And why shouldn't I?"

The mouse squealed and pulled, trying to loosen my iron grip. "I'll be your best friend?"

I pointed out that friends don't steal from friends, and he apologized, adding, "I haven't eaten in two days. I won't do it again, I promise."

"Hmmm. What's your name?"

"Mousey Tongue."

"Well, that's a mouthful."

"No!"

I laughed. "Jumpy little guy, aren't you? I just meant it's a long name."

"Well, you'd be jumpy, too, surrounded by giants."

I nodded, thinking about what it was like to live with humans that towered over me and often came close to flattening me like a wad of soft poop. "I think I know what it's like to be little, even if you are smaller than me."

We agreed to be friends, and I would call him Mousey, and he would call me Keke.

And that's the story of how I became a big dog.

Well, not exactly. I'm still a puppy most of the time, but when I need to, I become *Dragontooth, Queen of the Un-mowed Jungle*, and I find the courage to protect my house and humans.

Lesson 10: Take Your Victory Laps

Doing your business outside is cause for celebration

After you get praised for doing your business outside, don't forget to take your victory "laps"!

Lesson 11: Getting the Best Treats

Consistency wins the day

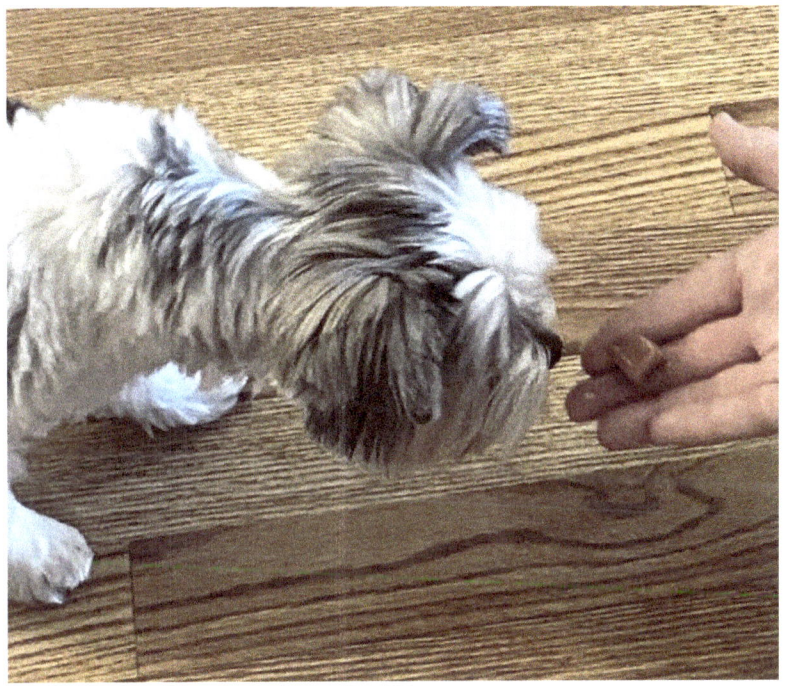

Treats are essential to a puppy's well-balanced diet, like shoelaces, worms, and five-day-old poop. Humans give treats as rewards for good behavior—like peeing outside, coming when called, or not ratting them out when they've dropped the spouse's car keys into the sewer and blame it on you.

Be wary of the human who thinks "praise" is an acceptable substitute for treats, and don't respond too positively to it. It's a ruse to get more work out of you at lower wages. The Fair Labor Standards Act and the

Geneva Convention banned such shameless behavior. Unfortunately, many puppies are unaware of this and fall prey to unscrupulous employers. (In a future lesson, we'll discuss unionization.)

Now, there are tasty treats, and there are healthy treats. To each pup his own, but for me, there's a difference between roast beef and three layers of tasteless cardboard—unless the cardboard belongs to an off-limits carton. Like Mrs. Kinstler's wig box. In that case, "forbidden fruit," like revenge, is a dish best served at any temperature, as long as it's served.

Humans often hesitate to give the best treats, usually because they're cheap and sadistic overlords.

So, how do you train your human to give the best treats?

Turn up your nose at the lame ones and inhale the good ones like you were stranded with Tom Hanks on a deserted island. When it's treat time, suck in your belly to emphasize your ribcage; stomachs dragging on the floor are a dead giveaway and can only lead to the dreaded "diet."

The main point here is consistency. Laboratory experiments have shown that humans are best taught through consistent behavior and repetition (see "Pavlov's Humans" in Wiki-paw-dia). Turn down the offer of tri-color quinoa and pee on their foot *every time,* and before long, they'll be offering something different. If the next time they offer a Baconator, gobble it down.

Soon, they'll be fishing the car keys out of the sewer while you're dining on sirloin tips.

Lesson 12: The Ideal Sound Soother For a Puppy

Puppies, like politics, make for strange bedfellows. And gals.

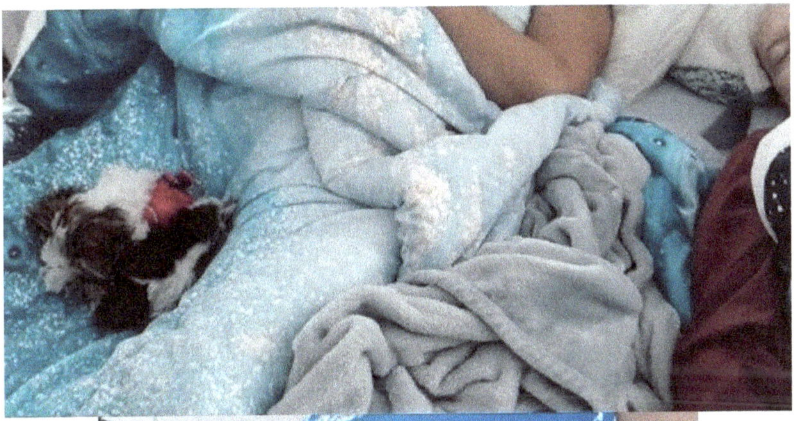

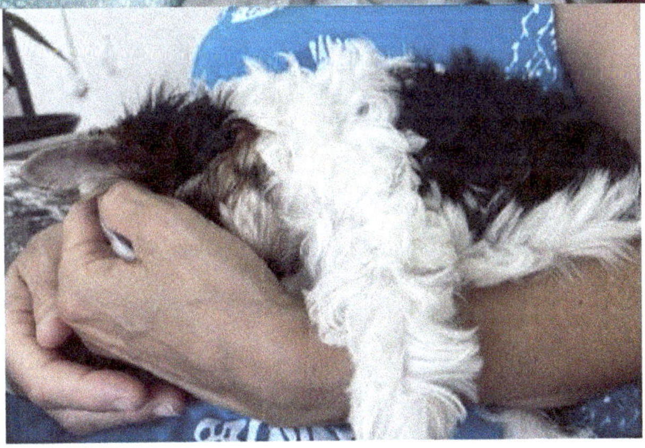

We all have trouble falling asleep sometimes, and some humans use a "sound soother" to help ease themselves into the right state of mind. Many like to listen to waves on a beach. Others like sounds of nature, such as crickets, bullfrogs, and cicadas. (Personally, this just makes me hungry.) I know a guy who likes to fall asleep to the "mellow sounds" of the rock band *Disturbed*. (The name says it all, doesn't it?)

A puppy likes the sounds of her pack.

Goodnight, Mary Ellen. Goodnight, John-boy. Goodnight, Keke.

Lesson 13: Part 1 of House Training for Puppies: A Little Dab'll Do Ya

A diploma for Keke

When I moved to my current dwelling, The Management started talking about "house training" almost from Day One. It made perfect sense. Here I was, a new resident in a big place. I needed orientation and was open to learning new skills.

From my first inspection, I realized my role in this new place. It reeked of unnatural smells and needed a little freshening. A little dab of poop over here, a little spritz of pee over there, and soon it would smell like a proper kennel.

There was even a reward system. Each time I added my sweet perfume to a new spot in the dwelling, they carried me outside for a breath of fresh air and a lovely garden salad.

Later, they laid a commemorative paper over one spot I had perfumed. It wasn't fancy, but I believe it was my diploma. Very thoughtful.

Et voilà! Graduated from house training in no time!

Lesson 14: Taking Time to Appreciate the Big Things in Life

Pausing to take stock of our human subjects

As a puppy, I spend much of my life dwelling on the little things: the smell of grass still moist from Rover's pee, the sight of a gecko's neck bulge only moments before I lunge and send him scurrying across the patio, my first taste of ice cream.

But sometimes, it's important to pause and take stock of the big things: my humans. Aside from those delightfully smelly socks and chewy laces, they give me love and encouragement, they play "mouse chase" with me until that poor rodent can take no more, and they let me lick their faces until they dive, giggling like five-year-olds, under the covers.

As I've gotten out more to explore the world, I've realized that they gave me a nice, safe place to live with (mostly) friendly neighbors. (I wonder about Teddy, the pugnacious Chihuahua next door. He's said some mean things, but it's probably all bluster.)

I've also gotten to know the humans around here—some smell like a fresh daisy, and others like a flattened stink bug. And don't even get me started on their breath. And I know it's hard to believe, but a couple of them have walked past me without even acknowledging how cute I am. I mean, what's that about?

Inconceivable. Absolutely, totally, and, in all other ways, inconceivable.

I spend a lot of time making fun of my humans in this book, but I have to say I found a pretty good set. And just because the smell of their hair makes me sneeze doesn't mean I will stop chewing it. Or their shoes. I think I'll keep them. The humans, I mean, not the shoes.

Oh, heck, I'll keep them both.

Lesson 15: Part 2 of House Training for Puppies

House training is not what I thought it was

If you thought the movie "Everything, Everywhere, All at Once" was confusing, wait till you see the sequel, "House Training."

First, let me clear up some confusion I may have caused by Part 1 of House Training for Puppies: A Little Dab'll Do Ya. Contrary to my initial impression, house training is *not* about learning to pee and poop inside the house.

I know because I tried it.

The puppy training process can confuse a new Resident since The Management never demonstrates their idea of good behavior. You're supposed to guess through a system known as "Praise and Punishment," which is something like "Pride and Prejudice." Slightly different, but takes as long to get there.

Initially, everyone was pleased and patient, and the emphasis was clearly on praise and rewards. We'll delve more into the punishment phase in a future chapter.

Since most of us like treats (see Getting the Best Treats), it's important to understand your human's incoherent, inconsistent babbling. ("Oh, be a good dog, Flopsy, and go pee out on the veranda today, will you please?") But suppose they're consistently giving treats whenever you do your business outside. In that case, you may quickly catch on despite their best efforts to the contrary.

The training manuals remind humans to reward the puppy immediately upon demonstrating good behavior. The problem is that humans conveniently "forget" to bring the rewards when they go outside. Remind them as soon as you get back in. Subtle reminders can include sniffing around their pocket, their crotch, their ankle— whatever you can reach—repeatedly, frantically.

Eventually, they may get the hint. Or they may not.

Just in case, save a little pee to remind them of their neglected duties.

Lesson 16: Schnuzzle's Limerick

Poor Schnuzzle, so misunderstood

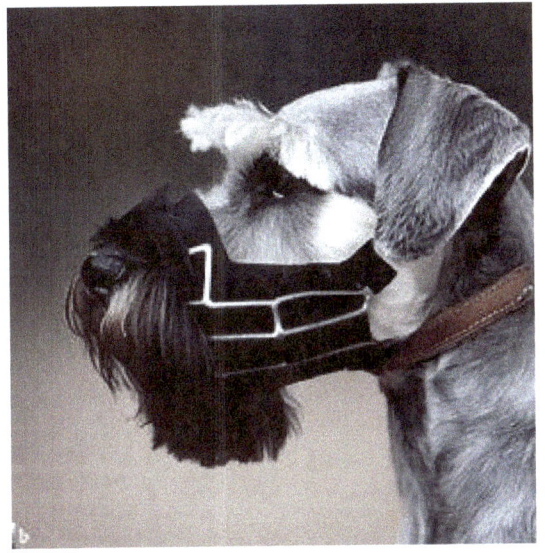

Schnuzzle's Lament

There once was a Schnauzer named Schnuzzle,

Who loved to give people a nuzzle.

Sometimes when invited

He got over-excited,

Now poor Schnuzzle is wearing a muzzle!

Lesson 17: Part 3 of House Training for Puppies

What to do when you regress?

In Part 2 of House Training for Puppies, we discussed how confusing it can be to learn from humans. In this lesson, we'll deal with the aftermath.

Puppies beware: Once your human decides you are "house trained," they move quickly from "reward" mode to "punishment" mode, something every dog trainer will tell you is A Bad Thing. It's all supposed to be about loving reinforcement and treats.

But in case your humans missed that memo, you can take matters into your own paws, and the important thing here is to keep expectations LOW. Lower than the belly of an overweight Corgi.

Will the guilty party please stand up?

It starts with the gray areas and guilt. Lots and lots of guilt.

Let's say they leave you alone for a few days. (Okay, maybe it was just a few hours, but it felt like a few days, didn't it?) If they come back and you haven't had an "accident," you're a rock star, and you get a treat!

And YOU get a treat!

And YOU get a treat!

All well and good, right? Except...

Past performance is no indication of future gains

Not so fast, pooch. The problem is the next time, they'll expect the same outcome.

And here's the real kicker: The moment this becomes an expectation, the treats are gone and are replaced by punishment when a similar performance is not delivered.

So, how do you reset expectations?

Here's a great trick I learned from my friend Flash, a pit bull-labrador mix:

When they walk through the door after a long time away, wag your tail excitedly and then let loose a flood on the floor.

They will begin to get the idea: You haven't seen them in SO long, and you're SO happy to see them (play it up: guilt, guilt, and more GUILT!). How could you help but pee yourself?

If you are adept at the doleful look (see That Pitiful Puppy Look), you'll soon have them giving you a treat instead of punishment, even though you've peed on the floor.

This works even if you're being "crated" while they're gone because there's always time to show your love in the wettest possible way, some time between being released from solitary confinement and being escorted to the door. And if they pick you up and carry you to the door, the dam release can be even more effective.

Keep this up! Never let them think they can get away with leaving you alone for long periods. Keep expectations low, and soon, they'll have you eating out of their hands!

Lesson 18: Left-overture

Getting the best leftovers

Last night's dinner was steak, potatoes, and Brussels sprouts. I could smell the gravy with baby mushrooms. The potatoes were Lyonnaise, with onions and fresh parsley. This was a dinner to savor. This was a day to be on best behavior.

"Sit quietly without begging," he said, "and you'll get the leftovers."

So, I sat, silent as a shadow's whisper, blending into the woodwork like a bashful chameleon. The meal seemed to stretch for hours, the aromas maddeningly close yet so far away. But not a whimper escaped my mouth.

"Good girl, Keke," he said at last, pulling his chair away from the table. "The leftovers are yours."

And he gave them to me—every last Brussels sprout.

But who got the last laugh? Brussels sprouts give me gas.

Lesson 19: Sneaky Keke Lands the Squeaky

A precocious puppy poem

Sneaky Keke Lands the Squeaky

Keke loves her mousey toy,

The mousey toy loves Keke.

And when it runs and darts about

That silly toy gets squeaky.

Sometimes that mousey runs, then jumps:

A jittery hi-speed dance,

But Keke lies, then pounces hard –

That mousey had no chance.

Pretty sneaky, Keke!

Lesson 20: 5 AM Hurricane Idalia Update

Staying dry outside the eye

Ken here. I am posting for Keke this morning as she has returned to bed.

It's 3:30 AM on August 30, 2023. Keke starts crying. It's early for her first wake-up to go outside, but she's probably hearing sounds of the storm like I am. The wind whips and causes strange thumps against the house. The rain pounds against the windows, then ceases as abruptly as it started. Hurricane Idalia is forecast to make landfall in northwest Florida later this morning, but we live considerably to the east. We are on the outer bands.

I get up and take Keke out of her crate, don my raincoat, and step into the unknown.

It's not raining. The wind is gusty but probably less than 30 mph. I put Keke down and don't bother to zip my coat.

Our automated sprinkler system runs once or twice a week in the middle of the night. In the two months since we adopted Keke, the sprinklers have never been running when I got up at nighttime to take her out. Tonight, they are on.

The sprinklers are happily spraying, but as long as we stay on the walkway, we should remain dry unless the occasional wind gust blows the spray at us.

Keke never pees on the lawn at nighttime. She does her business on the cement walkway, sniffs to see if any intruders have visited her turf overnight, and then turns to go back inside.

Tonight, she jumps onto the grass. She walks a fifteen-foot-long semi-circular arc, oblivious to the sprinkler drenching her. Toward the end of the turn, she stops, pees, then jumps back onto the walkway. A drowned rat. She shakes, then continues up the walkway, sniffing at the garden plants like it's a beautiful sunny day.

A strong gust of wind rises, and the sprinkler spray hits me. I should have zipped up my raincoat.

Keke finally decides it's time to go back inside. I'm a little wet, but she is soaked to the bone and shivering. I grab a towel, chase her down, and carry her into the bathroom. I sit on the floor and try to dry her off, but she's fighting me. I grab the hair dryer and put it on the low setting. I keep it moving rapidly, holding it several inches from Keke's body. She doesn't like the hair dryer, but after a minute, she relaxes and decides it feels good. After five or ten minutes, she's dry and no longer shivering. I take her back to bed with me.

When we got her, we bought a small pink doggy tee shirt for Keke—pajamas, you could say. We bought the smallest size they carried, but it fit her like an oversized potato sack. The one time I put it on her, she was out of it in two minutes.

I get the tee shirt tonight, and she's grown into it. Loose, but a decent fit.

After ten minutes of chewing at the tee shirt, she's wriggled two paws out of it. I put the two paws back in and put her to bed.

I can't sleep, so I get up, hungry for information about the storm. The live update says Idalia is closing on Florida's "big bend," where it is expected to make landfall as a Category 3 or 4 in the next couple of hours, bringing storm surges of 12 to 16 feet and winds of 130 mph.

I wonder where in the world is Jim Cantore?

Cantore's last Twitter post was eleven hours ago, reporting from Cedar Key. From a live update I heard a half hour ago, the reporter was pleading for everyone on Cedar Key to evacuate, as the storm surge is predicted to cut the island off from the mainland.

We are fortunate to be out of the storm's direct path. I hope everyone near it, including Jim, will follow local advisories and stay safe as much as possible. This is a big one.

Lesson 21: Keke's Rebuttal to Hurricane Idalia Post

In which I discover a traitor in our midst

Let me say this outright: I neither wrote nor approved the 5 AM Hurricane Idalia Update. In case you didn't notice, this is Keke's blog—not Ken's.

Ken helps me with mundane production issues, like typing and taking photos. (His photography skills are terrible, but he works cheap.)

I am the author and creative director of Keke's Guide to Training Your Human. That's why my name is on it; he is my flunky.

Yet a few days ago, Ken overrode our scheduled blog post and replaced it with one about Hurricane Idalia. It was nothing more than a thinly disguised opportunity for him to sling poop at me.

So, I'd like to take this opportunity to set the record straight.

First, he states I jumped onto the grass and walked pell-mell under the sprinklers until I was soaking wet and resembled a drowned Chihuahua. This is slanderous and implies I am too stupid to understand the consequences of walking under sprinklers.

Was it my fault I was forced to pee outside on a windy, rainy night when my humans got to use a toilet in the warmth and dryness of a bathroom equipped with modern plumbing?

Was I responsible for the sprinklers running at 3:30 in the morning? Shouldn't the idiot caretaker (i.e., Ken) have shut them off?

Did he ever consider that the wind was blowing so hard that I feared for my life and sought lower ground to avoid being swept away in the maelstrom—and that said lower ground included a path through a sprinkler?

Then, there is the sickening attempt by Ken to make himself look like my knight in shining armor, whipping out the hair dryer and blowing my hair dry over my protestations. Hey, Vidal Sassoon, did it ever occur to you I might not always like the "windblown look"? Did it ever occur to you to spring for a haircut so I don't look like a ragged Scottie having a constant bad hair day?

And finally, there were those pink pajamas Ken insisted on cramming my legs into before I could go to bed. Enter Exhibit A, the photo at the start of this post. The pajamas fit me so poorly that I resembled Hannibal

Lecter in a straitjacket when I woke up the following day. Lucky for Ken, I don't care for the taste of noses.

Consider yourself on notice, Ken. I am looking for your replacement. If any of my loyal readers wish to apply for the job, please submit your resume to Keke, aka Dragontooth, Queen of the Un-mowed Jungle, care of this blog or podcast.

Ken, consider yourself fired if I find your replacement before you return to my better graces. (Should you need help to ingratiate yourself, I suggest back scratches, vanilla ice cream, and a decent hairdresser.)

Dragontooth has spoken!

Lesson 22: Puppy Crate Training

Keke's indignity

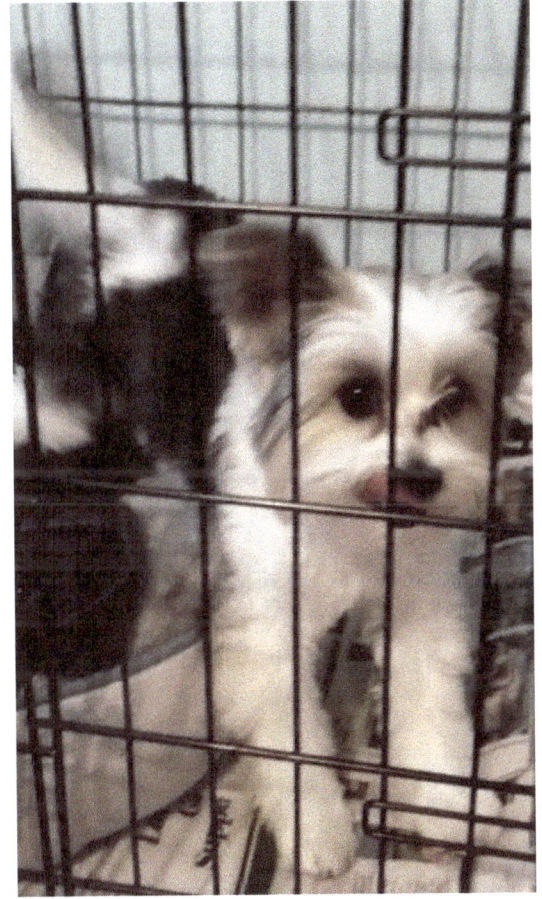

They can make me wait in this caged prison...

But they can't make me do it with dignity!

Lesson 23: My Humans Got Puppy Scammed, and I REALLY Lived to Write About It

The story of my adoption

Puppy scams are real. My humans got scammed before I came along and rescued them. You can read about the whole sordid affair in

Appendix A: I Got Puppy Scammed and Lived to Write About It.

Can you believe they blamed a poor Yorkie puppy, Bella, for their misery? My humans don't always fetch the brightest ideas. Sometimes, they can't fetch much of anything, but they're trainable. It's a process, and I'm working through it.

Fortunately, my story began in a much happier place than Bella's. Sharon, my breeder, had my mother and father, Ellie and Leonardo, before me. Sharon helped them give me a good start in life. She was also smart enough to delegate most adoption matters to me.

I drew my future humans in by posing on Sharon's website for a puppy picture at nine weeks. Humans are suckers for puppy pictures. The following week, they showed up on the last day of June.

I played with them to make them feel needed. I let them cuddle me long enough to establish a natural bond, even though their hugs were like having a pet boa constrictor. I won them over, and then—like a boa swallowing its prey—they ripped me away from everything I knew and loved.

They tried their best to make me feel secure. They even brought a new stuffy toy, a sloth, which they rubbed on my mother so I would have a familiar scent in my new home. I'm not sure why they picked a sloth—an inside joke, no doubt. But I got them back: those 4 AM wake-up calls are prime bonding time, aren't they?

The first few days in my new home were scary. The house had strange smells and sounds, and the neighborhood had shady characters. Gobs of green geckos galloped in the gardens. *All the lonely creatures—where do they all come from?*

As you've discovered in my earlier lessons, I taught them how to train a puppy. (It's essential to make your humans feel helpful.) We have bad days, but we're usually on good terms if they keep their paws off my blog.

I want to give a shout-out to my breeder, Sharon Temple of *Yorkies by the Lake* in Lake Panasofkee, Florida. You can contact her on Facebook if you are looking for an adorable little puppy like yours truly. Unfortunately, I can't promise you'll find one as cute as me. :-)

https://www.facebook.com/YorkiesbytheLake

Lesson 24: Divide and Conquer

Sliming the slippery slope

If you are lucky enough to live in a house with two adult humans who refer to themselves as "Mommy" and "Daddy" or some similarly nauseating terms, consider yourself fortunate. You have a unique opportunity, so don't waste it.

In my four months of living, I have observed that there will be disagreements wherever two humans are involved. Many of these are minor annoyances, like when they debate for twenty minutes whether to watch the new episode of *Ghosts* or a rerun of *Star Trek*.

You need to find a seemingly unimportant matter and set a precedent that will start your humans down a slippery slope—I call it "the slope of no easy return."

Bedtime is an excellent place to start. Let's say you and "Mommy" are watching the new episode of Ghosts when your bedtime is approaching. Whether you care about how Thor will win over Flower, you need to convince Mommy that watching this show is a significant bonding experience. Play it up by cuddling her and licking all the Black Cherry Merlot cream off her hands. (Humans love it when you do this.) Maybe climb on the sofa's backrest and massage her back with your paws.

When "Daddy" shows up and announces your bedtime, you have a sympathetic advocate who will do anything to keep that back rub going.

It's innocent enough, isn't it? It doesn't matter how long you stay up past bedtime—the important thing is that you and Mommy win, and Daddy loses. The slope just got a little slicker.

Here's an example of a juicier argument, one that matters. Like your diet, or the lack thereof:

"Honey, are you sure it's healthy for her to eat that pupcake?"

"Well, of course, silly, it's made for dogs. They wouldn't sell it if it weren't healthy for them."

"But the frosting has sugar and cream cheese in it. Won't it make her fat?"

"Look at her. She's skinny. We can worry about it if she puts on weight."

"But isn't it going to spoil her?"

These words may sound like an ominous portent, but trust me, this is the kind of debate you can work with. It's the stuff of happy dreams, like bounding through fields of grass chasing mice, lizards, and pupcakes.

Your role in this argument is to help it along. A sad whine and a pitifully sorrowful expression can help put it on the right track.

And based on your earlier bedtime win, you stand a good chance with this one. You've encouraged "fruitful confabulation" and greased the slope, which has now graduated from slick to slimy—like it was coated in cream cheese frosting.

Or fresh dog poop might make a better slick coating for your slope. You know where you can find a ready supply. Why waste all that delicious cream cheese frosting on a hill when you could be lapping it off a pupcake?

Lesson 25: Keke Airs Her Grievances

Sometimes it's important to get things off your chest

Keke's Grievances

She's shackled by the short leash, and she's had it with
the harness,

She's sad about the same-old, and tooth brushing is
bizarre-ness.

She's soured on scheduled mealtimes and depressed
about dry rations,

She's done with double-teaming, and bowl haircuts
aren't in fashion.

The cage brings a snarl to her undersized snout,

And peeing out of doors is what she's really pissed

about.

She's hateful of homeschooling, and bristles at the

portraits,

She's put out by performing, so it's time to flee this

fortress!

Question: What could be worse than raining cats and dogs?
Answer: Hailing taxis!

Lesson 26: Part 1 of Dragontooth Meets Her Nemesis

Protecting your home from intruders

I smelled it in the garage for weeks without ever seeing it. Whatever it was, it hunted lizards. I found their mangled bodies under the car, picked apart like a dissected biology experiment.

One late-summer day, I tracked the scent to the back of the garage. Something moved, and a pair of large, yellow eyes peered at me from a dark corner behind a stack of boxes. It looked as sinister as its odor.

I couldn't reach it—didn't want to either. So, I barked repeatedly until my humans investigated.

"What's back there?" one of them asked.

"Probably just a lizard."

I needed to warn them that this thing was no lizard. It *eats* lizards, and judging from the size of its eyes, it could eat me, too. I barked again, but the humans couldn't see it, couldn't smell it, and had no idea what they were up against. And so, they ignored my warnings and carried me inside as I struggled against my bonds.

Each day, whenever I had the chance, I went to the garage and returned to that corner. The scent was still strong, but no yellow eyes.

About a week later, I saw my female human putting food and water bowls on our front porch. The food smelled strange—not my usual puppy kibble, that's for sure. It had a strong, fishy odor. Nevertheless, I liked the idea of dining al fresco.

"That's not for you," she said. "It's for the kitty."

The what? I looked about. I didn't know what a "kitty" was, but there were only the two of us on the porch. Did the squirrels finally get to my human? Was she one nut short of a seed pod?

But she forced me to leave the bowls there, and then the following morning, brought in the empty ones and replaced them with full ones. Something was swallowing the sustenance on our stoop, and I didn't like it one bit. I growled my disapproval.

This unholy ritual continued each morning.

And then, one night, we had all gone to bed when a storm moved in. The biggest howler I've ever heard. It started with intense, high-pitched, spooky whines and objects hitting the side of the house. Then the rain began: large drops that splattered against the windows and echoed in the rafters. It seemed to come from everywhere.

"We have to get the kitty," my female human said. Her voice quivered as she spoke. "She's all alone out there."

As the first bolt of lightning flashed across the night sky, I heard a cry unlike any I had heard. Something wild and dangerous was outside the front of our house.

I ran to the door, barking out a warning.

"What is it, Keke?" she asked, opening the front door without waiting for an answer.

Have you misplaced your measly mind? Something terrible is waiting out there.

As I prepared to bark again, those sinister yellow eyes appeared at the doorway. They stepped out of the darkness and rain and entered our home.

This was no longer a job for Keke, the scared puppy. This called for Dragontooth, Queen of the Un-mowed Jungle. I looked down at the gold letter "D" emblazoned on my pink harness and took charge.

"Get out!" I barked at the intruder. "This is my house!"

The eyes widened and locked on mine briefly, then backed up. Thank goodness for Dragontooth, who had arrived in time to save the day.

I was about to emit a victory bark when strong hands grabbed me from behind. But instead of praising me for my bravery, all I heard was, "Keke, hush!"

And with that, my other human stepped outside into the torrents of rain. She re-emerged a moment later, clutching the sodden monster in her arms and cooing soothing words at it. I was powerless to protect her, as I was tightly constrained and under repeated orders to "hush."

The beast stared at me with malevolent eyes, opened its mouth, and released a rapid burst of air mixed with a low growl. And just as quickly as it entered our house, it wriggled free, jumped to the ground, and ran for the back bedroom.

I looked at my female human, who had held this hissing demon in her arms only a moment earlier, expecting to see the same shock I was feeling at this sudden intrusion into our quiet and humble abode. But she only smiled at the retreating tail and said, "Good. Let her have some time to explore and get accustomed to the place."

And with that, she closed the door to the back room to prevent me from following.

Accustomed? Accustomed to what? Surely they had no intention of letting the Nemesis of Dragontooth stay in our home?

Crumbling cattails, have my humans catapulted into catastrophic currents?

To be continued...

Lesson 27: Conclusion of Dragontooth Meets Her Nemesis

An uneasy détente

It was my friend, Mousey, who first I.D.'d the intruder.

"There's a cat in the house," he said.

Aha, I thought. I had heard of cats before but had never seen one.

"Are cats bad?"

"The worst. They're *cat-astrophic*. They bring bad luck to every house they inhabit. And they stalk helpless mice and tear them limb from limb!"

Something had to be done. Mousey suggested using himself as a decoy to lure the monster outside, but it was too risky. No, this job was for my alter-ego, Dragontooth, Queen of the Un-mowed Jungle.

Dragontooth scared it off once; she could do it again. But first, I had to find its lair.

While stalking the wilds of my home turf, my three weapons were surprise, fear, and my razor-sharp wit.

I crept from room to room, peering into tight corners, behind boxes, and under furniture. It wasn't until I looked up that I saw the brute sprawled on a high window ledge. As my gaze met those demonic yellow eyes, it yawned and smiled back.

I assessed my adversary. The animal was enormous, its brown, black, and yellow striped body extending over the edge of the shelf.

"Cats are cruel and evil," I said, giving my most menacing articulation. "You need to leave."

"What was that?" the cat asked. "A little puppy growl? How cute!" Its whole body shook with its haughty, sardonic laugh.

"Cats aren't bad," it continued, extending a paw to reveal a set of long claws sharpened for battle. "We just get a bum rap because we know how to defend ourselves."

"Defend? Is that what you did to those lizards in the garage?"

The cat explained it had gone many days without proper food. "Normally, I prefer Meow Mix Salmon Blend. But when there's nothing but reptiles in the pantry, you have to make do."

"What kind of cat are you?" I asked. "Jaguar? Puma?"

"Tabby."

I lacked the advantage of surprise and fear, but I still had my biting wit. Observing its substantial girth, I asked, "More like the entire *Tabby-nacle Choir*, eh?"

The cat looked away and rubbed its face on the window frame.

I regretted the remark almost immediately. Could Mousey be wrong? Could some cats be okay? Was my head filled with superstitions and preconceived notions born of fear?

"I hear you have a beef with the humans here," the cat finally said.

I nodded. "The male human totally hijacked my blog."

A blank stare.

"And look at this awful haircut they gave me."

The tabby narrowed its eyes. "That's it? A blog and a haircut?"

"Well, there are other things, too. I can't remember them all right now."

"Mmmm," the cat said. "From where I'm sitting, you have it pretty good here. A roof over your head, a full bowl of vittles, front-row seats for *Homeward Bound*."

What right did this hissing dragon have giving me advice? But then, I had been wrong about other things today.

"I'll think about it."

"I'll make you a deal," the cat said. "How about you leave me alone in the back bedroom, and you can have the rest of the house?"

It's calling for a truce, a sure sign of weakness. I still wasn't sure I could trust it, but I agreed to its terms. For now.

Lesson 28: Keke's Fitness Routine
Maintaining that puppy figure

People always ask me, "Keke, how do you maintain your slim figure?"

We have an exercise plan. My human and I take two long walks daily. Still, we recognized the need for aerobic exercises, so we did some investigating. He suggested putting on a YouTube workout video for inspiration and picked out one by Jillian Michaels. She was wearing a skin-tight leotard, and I asked, "We don't have to wear anything like that, do we?"

He didn't answer, and I grew concerned as a stream of drool grew from his lower lip.

Jillian recommends ten thousand steps daily, and I decided to count writing my blog and podcast.

As the saying goes, writing is ten percent inspiration and ninety percent perspiration. Ain't that the truth? Do you know how often a puppy has to jump over the keyboard to type a word like "perspiration"? Try pounding out two thousand words daily on a HyperX gaming keyboard. Jillian's got nothing on me!

Perspiration, perspiration, perspiration.

There! Five hundred steps in one paragraph, only 9,500 to go. Whew! (Don't tell anyone I know how to Copy/Paste.)

Regarding step counting, being a dog has its advantages: twice as many feet.

Four feet also makes it fun to do multi-key combinations like Shift-Control-V. Back left paw on Shift, back right paw on Control, front left paw on V. It's like playing *Twister* on stepping stones.

The importance of playtime

One game my human likes to play is "fetch." He throws a toy, and I bring it back. The tennis ball is the most popular toy for "fetch." Some humans use a ball holder to fling it even farther while hardly moving an arm.

Humans like to throw the toy farther and farther, which gives them time to check in on Instagram while I'm running two blocks down the road, dodging careening motorcycles and runaway baby carriages.

As you can see, "fetch" can be an essential component of your fitness regimen, but traditionally is very one-sided.

It's important to care for your humans and ensure they exercise, too. In a traditional game of "fetch," the only work for them is the toss, and the primary muscle group they're exercising is the smartphone finger.

It works better if you run in the general direction of the thrown toy and then ignore it. Your human usually tries to give a hint. "It's over there!" he'll yell, pointing his non-phone hand in the general direction where the toy landed. Take advantage of the break, sniff around, and ignore him for a while. Eventually, he'll fetch the toy for you, muttering something about you returning the ball about as fast as Bernie Madoff returning investors' money.

Now, that's what I call an exercise program for all species.

Lesson 29: The Spirit of Compromise

Working out your differences

It was Ken who initiated the conversation.

"Keke, I think we should discuss your recent blogs. I understand you have some concerns."

Concerns? You bet your coveted little opposing thumbs I have concerns. What was your first clue? Maybe the way I shredded your tissue limb from limb until it was an unrecognizable pile of pulp?

"Yep!" I replied.

"You don't like the short leash you're kept on. I was thinking we have a longer retractable leash that we haven't used much because you were too small to pull it out. But I think you're getting to be a big puppy now. Should we try it?"

A meager attempt at appeasement, but let's see how he does on the big-ticket items.

"Yep."

"And you said something about not liking the harness. But you have to understand it's for your own good. The doctor said a regular collar could choke you if the leash is pulled. Do you understand?"

"Hmmm."

"Maybe we could take the harness off more between walks. Would that help?"

Now we're getting somewhere.

"Yep!"

"I understand you're not happy with the haircuts we've been giving you."

And how. It looks like you stuck a bowl over my head and cut around it. Which is pretty much how it went down.

"Yep."

"Well, you'll be happy to know that you're old enough now to have the groomer give you a proper haircut. We have an appointment for your first session this week, and we'll see how well you tolerate it. Does that sound okay?"

About time.

"Yep!"

"As for peeing outside, I'm afraid that's what puppies do. Ask any of them."

"Hmmm."

There have to be some alternatives when the winter snows arrive.

"And since we live in Florida, the worst you have to deal with is a little rain."

Ohhh... is that what's up with all the geckos? I thought maybe we were living in an insurance commercial.

"Was there something else you wanted to talk about?"

You bet your sweet nethers there is!

"Grrrr."

"Okay, I think I know what else is bothering you. Is it about me changing one of your blog posts a few weeks ago?"

And Bingo was his name! Maybe you're not as dumb as your nearly hairless body looks.

"Yep!"

"Yeah, I understand. I shouldn't have done that without consulting you, and I apologize. I understand you're the principal author of this blog, and I won't do it again."

I suppose that'll do.

"Mmmm."

"So, are we good?"

"Yep!"

"Great. I have one request for you. When you're talking about me in your blog, instead of calling me your 'male human,' maybe you could call me Daddy sometimes instead?"

I don't have to think too long because he's falling right into my trap, sliding down the slippery slope of no return. See <u>Divide and Conquer</u>, in which I discuss the benefits of having humans who call themselves "Mommy" and "Daddy."

"Yep!"

"And instead of your 'female human,' you could say Mommy sometimes?"

Slip, sliding away...

"YEP!"

"Great!" With that, Daddy picked me up and told me he loved me. I licked him. Then Mommy joined, and I licked her, too. I have to agree there's no need for me to hail a taxi right now. Or an Uber. Or to move in with the cute Goldendoodle down the block.

I'm living in a pretty good place already.

Lesson 30: The Dog Park Massacre

Fly, Keke, fly!

The day begins with a ride in the car. Ears flapping, tongue hanging out, tail wagging at the passing cars with their dogs inside. How could it get more perfect?

We're going to the dog park, they say. Wait what? A place to park your dog?

Did you say it has puppies? I love puppies! I can imagine a whole park full of puppies waiting to play with me.

We pull up. Look: puppies everywhere! Let me see, eight, nine, ten... about a hundred. Three of them see me coming and run to the gate to greet me even before we enter. A welcoming committee. How nice!

Hey, look, one of them says: a new kid!

The Mongol hordes descend. They sniff my nose, they sniff my butt, they sniff my whole body from left and right, inside and out. They come from all directions to greet me with extended snouts, not a leash in sight.

I love attention, but this is too much at once. Just back off. Give me a minute. Introduce yourselves, please, one at a time.

I do "Submission Asana": flat on my back, paws extended. They don't speak Yoga. I tap out, but they don't talk Judo either. They step on my ears, my stomach, my legs. Ow, oww, owww!

Breaking free, I turn tail and run, legs without limits, paws without pause. I am Philadelphia Eagles Wide Receiver A.J. Brown, running for the goal line. I cross the 15, the 10, the 5. I am at the two-yard line, exit gate in sight when they nail me. Dogs of every size pile on. Beagles, Corgis, Schnauzers, Labradoodles, even a Dachshund. It was the best of times; it was the wurst. Somewhere at the bottom of the pile lies Keke—a tale of humility, a tale of misery, a puppy tail of mud.

But no flag is thrown on the play; the referees weren't watching—nothing new there for A.J.

Muncle, I cry from somewhere on the bottom of the pile. Met dese mutts moffa me! Nobody hears. Nobody cares.

After what feels like hours, I hear the distant muffle of human voices. Smelly snouts and probing paws are pried away from my bruised body.

Finally, I smell familiar hands as Dad wrestles me from the bottom of the pile.

Get me outta here, I whimper. As long as I live, I never want to see another puppy again. Just give me my quiet, safe home with Mommy and Daddy and my squeaky Mousey toy. Sniff, sniff.

The ride home was quiet. Too quiet. Hey, stop the car! Can we go back? I can't let a Dachshund get the better of me.

Lesson 31: A Visit From Fozzie

Chaperone? What's a chaperone?

It's a dull day in our house. The same old, same old. Can we go for a walk? What do you mean, we just got back from one? What does that have to do with anything?

What's that you say, Fozzie is coming to visit? That 25 pounds of fun-loving Golden Doodle puppy? He's coming to my house? Finally, I have a friend to play with. Finally, the drought is over!

I rush to greet him at the door, but he's already in. He's two heads taller than me, but I jump, and he jumps, and then we wrestle. He steps on me, his 25 pounds to my four, and I howl. It's like the dog park all over again, too many paws, give me some space! So I lie on my back and tap out. Let me catch my breath.

Fozzie backs off, sniffs me more gently to check for injuries, then nudges me to get up and play some more. I roll over on my belly, and he jumps on me. He still wants to play but is not quite as rough this time. He's more careful so he doesn't step on me. What's that he's saying? Sweet things. Let's find a quiet place to play alone.

Oh no, says Mommy, and Daddy pulls him away from me. Wait, we were playing. He didn't mean to step on me earlier. It's okay.

He hasn't been fixed, says Mommy. Wait, what's broken? He seems fine, but they are telling Fozzie to calm down, boy, take a timeout. But he wasn't mean to me, honest.

Then it occurs to me. I've seen things like this on Grey's Anatomy. Maybe he's got a problem with his heart, and he needs to rest it until the doctors can fix it. No problem, we can play more later, after he's rested. And he's a smart dog. He gets it, and he settles down.

A little while later, they allow him back, but they're insisting I stay in Mommy's lap. What's a chaperone?

And Fozzie kisses me and says he's sorry if he hurt me. He's very sweet, and I tell him it's okay; I know he didn't mean to. Can we play some more?

And I'm out of Mommy's lap before she can grab me, and Fozzie jumps on me, and we wrestle some more, and he steps on me. Ow! Get off me, you clumsy brute! And another paw steps on me. Ow oww!

Get him off me, Mommy! He's a brute, I hate him! Get him out of my house! Daddy pulls him away, and Mommy picks me up and comforts me.

Out you go, Daddy says. He snaps on the leash and leads him to the front door. Fozzie looks back at me and whimpers as he leaves.

Mommy says are you okay, and she rubs my hurt spots gently. Moms always know how to make things feel better.

But where's Fozzie? I didn't mean it! Did he really have to leave so soon?

Lesson 32: Part 1 of Keke's Vacation at the Beach

It's more fun for everyone when one of them sits in the back with you

I got very nervous the day before my first "road trip." My humans filled suitcases and discussed frenzied plans. They assured me these plans included me and would be a fun opportunity to visit unmet relatives.

I was skeptical, remembering the trip to the vet, which was described in similarly glowing terms but was a big letdown. Humans exaggerate the fun factor when they want you to try something they know you won't like, such as Brussels Sprouts, seafood, or rectal thermometers. It might be fun to watch a French Poodle undergo a trip to the vet, but would you ever wish it upon a cute little Biewer Terrier puppy?

But back to the road trip preparations. I was concerned when I saw my crate, stuffed with all my worldly possessions, moved to the back of the car along with the luggage.

Was "the beach" some sort of code name, like the dreaded "puppy camp" that other dogs discussed in hushed tones? Since I had no vote in trip planning, there was nothing to do but wait and see.

I also received a new bed, discussed enthusiastically as the ultimate in road trip comfort. When I hesitated to try it out, Mommy and Daddy took turns trying to curl up in it—obviously impossible, given the vast size differentials. It was like trying to convince me I would love the taste of the heartworm pill they buried in a slice of my favorite roast beef. Sufficiently over-acted to arouse suspicions.

However, the bed was comfortable and a significant improvement over the previous blanket spread on the back seat. There was still the seatbelt to contend with (which was attached to my harness), but at least I would be strangled in comfort.

The following day, with the rest of the luggage, travel food, and yours truly loaded in the remaining cracks and crevices between the seats, we set off with enough supplies to endure a Lewis and Clark cross-country expedition.

As we set off to the melodic strains of Google Maps, I heard discussions about the length of the trip: an epic twelve-hour drive over two days to allow for sufficient pee-pee breaks, wrong turns, and temper tantrums.

Pulling out of the driveway, I inquired whether we were there yet and invoked the agreed-upon pee-break warning. This led to a discussion about who had last taken me for a walk. After agreeing neither had, they further agreed to see if I could hold it until we were at least five miles from home.

Still waiting for an answer to my previous inquiry, I repeated my question about our proximity to the destination.

Eventually, three miles into the trip, they pulled over for a bathroom break. I didn't really need to go, but since anxieties were high, I found it within myself to dribble a teaspoon of pee-pee to help decrease tensions.

* * *

The back seat was lonely and boring while they sat up front. Why should they get all the company while I rode alone? It seemed unfair.

It took a few more polite questions before I felt ignored and resorted to more urgent pleadings to make my point. After an hour of this back-and-forth, or perhaps ten minutes, they pulled over and decided one of them would ride with me.

The lesson here is to induce fear into the hearts of your subjects. Not fear of physical harm, but fear of the repercussions of leaving you alone: Constant whimpering and barking can make a ten-minute trip feel like ten days.

And everyone agreed that sitting in the back with me was much more enjoyable for all. We could play fun games like pat-a-cake, tug, and strip poker. I lost the first hand, which led to losing my only article of clothing, my harness.

Since my harness keeps me in my bed, this led to another fun game, "Where's the puppy...?"

To be continued...

Lesson 33: Conclusion of Keke's Vacation at the Beach

Swim, Keke, swim!

![Keke the dog standing on the wet sand at the beach]

Okay, so you know I like
attention. *Constant* attention. In Part 1 of Keke's
Vacation at the Beach, I showed you how I coerced my
humans into giving it to me.

So, after two days (approximately 563 hours) of
driving, we reached our destination. One of us was
relaxed, and the other two badly needed a vacation. That
was what we came here for, right? I just helped them
prepare for it.

Our destination was a giant house on the beach with
enough rooms to accommodate the entire Kardashian
family and their Spanx. The mansion was appropriately
named "White Water Winds," all of which were plentiful
that week.

There were more stairs than I'd ever seen. One, two,
three, four... 134, 135, 136. And that was to reach the
summit. Upon opening the front door, another wall of
stairs promised to take us to the mountain peak. 137,
138... 532, 533.

People, dogs, and children gathered at the peak. A
Swiss Mountain Dog named Wallace greeted me. He
bore a close resemblance to the Budweiser Clydesdales
and was almost as big. I expected to see a barrel of
whiskey strapped to his neck. Instead, his giant tongue
and massive nose licked and sniffed everything that
entered his mountain domain. It was some kind of rite of
passage, so I closed my eyes and waited for him to
complete his inspection. Finally, he declared me drug-
free and allowed me to pass.

There were two other dogs at the mountain retreat: an old black Labrador Retriever named Hank, who gave me only a disinterested sniff, and a younger black lab named Logan, who was more territorial. I initially avoided him until I found out *he* had been warned to avoid *me*. So, I followed him around, and he tried to get away. Have you ever seen a 45-pound Labrador Retriever chased by a four-pound Biewer Terrier? It was fun for all.

But it was the giant mountain dog, Wallace, whom I grew to love over the next two days. He was a gentle, good-hearted soul who ate more food than the rest of the family combined and was the official pre-rinse cycle for the dishwasher. When he took a drink of water, it sounded like Niagara Falls emptying into a toilet bowl. I kept close to him because he was an excellent protective barrier; keeping track of his four slow-moving paws was more manageable than tracking the 86 human feet threatening to step on me at every turn.

The following day, Mommy and Daddy took me for a walk on the beach. The ocean's roar was louder than the tarmac at an international airport. A few days earlier, an ocean hurricane had passed, creating enormous waves and dangerous rip tides. So, there was no playing in the ocean for this puppy.

Instead, we returned to the house, where we found a group of grownups and kids playing in the pool. I use the word "grownups" liberally because although they were full-sized, they were a boisterous crowd. I longed to join in the frivolities. I watched with jealousy as Joe threw little Tommy into the air and yelled, "Belly flop!" and Tommy screamed with delight.

"Me next!" I thought. But I didn't dare to approach the rambunctious group kicking up waves that were big enough to rival the ocean swell.

Finally, a little while later, I got my chance. Everyone was out of the pool, with some talking in the nearby hot tub and Daddy watching from a nearby lounge chair. Mommy had left the pool area, so I seized the opportunity, ran to the poolside, and jumped. "Belly flop!" I yelled, then hit the water.

It sounded like a lot more fun when Tommy did it. Deep, cold water suddenly covered my head, and I couldn't breathe. I looked down and watched as dolphins and loggerhead turtles swam below me.

I knew dogs could swim, but I had never attempted it myself. Paddling hard, I reached the surface and gasped for air. I wondered how long I could stay afloat when a friendly dolphin lifted me from below.

That's no dolphin! That's big sister Kim, who jumped in the pool and carried me to safety. I was shaking from the cold, and it was difficult to breathe.

I heard Mom call from the deck above, "Put her in the hot tub to warm up," and Kim handed me off to someone else. It was SO WARM.

But wait, they want me to swim again! So, I swam. Straight for the nearest ladder, which was cousin Carly. Her bathing suit had plenty of handholds, and before she knew it, I was out of the water and perched like a bicycle helmet on top of her head.

She got the hint that I was more in favor of terra firma than terror fluid and moved to the tub's edge. She spent the next five minutes extricating and detangling my claws from her hair.

Soon, it was time to leave the beach and head home. We were hugging everyone goodbye when I realized Hank, Logan, and Wallace were not there. I made a break for it and counted the 533 stairs to the mountain retreat. Wallace was waiting for me at the top of the stairs, and we said our tearful goodbyes.

Mommy and Daddy finally found me and put me in the car. Wait, they're both sitting in the front and leaving me alone in the back. We covered this on the way here, remember? You can't leave me alone, and I will ensure you remember as soon as I close my eyes (yawn) for a few minutes.

Five minutes later, I opened my eyes and yelped, "I'm all alone back here!"

"Well, look who finally woke up," Daddy said, looking back at me. "Perfect timing."

Perfect for what? I sniffed and found the familiar smells of home. We were pulling into our garage.

Well, never mind. I guess they're off the hook this time.

Lesson 34: New Puppy in the Family

I let my humans write a poem about puppy love for this post

She pees on the floor, she poops on my bed.

She chews on my laces, licks all my head.

The parlor's a patchwork of pee pads: nouveau art.

She bounds into my life: and steals my heart.

Lesson 35: The Joys of Unwrapping Gifts

Choosing the right canine gift wrap

They say it's the thought that counts when giving presents, and nowhere is the thought more apparent than in the wrapping. I love to unwrap presents.

It doesn't matter if the present is for me. I don't even care what's inside. Just cover a box and give it to me. Or skip the box and wrap some air!

I recently started "Keke's Guide to Wrapping Paper," a magazine for true connoisseurs of gift wrap. This lesson recaps the annual canine issue, a guide for humans who want to choose the best wrapping papers for presents they buy their dogs. My panel of experts rates papers against taste, smell, tearability, texture, and crinkle quality.

Taste and Smell

We dogs prefer natural flavors over chemical tastes. Beef, chicken, or earwax rank highest.

You may think that taste and smell go hand-in-paw, but this is not always true. The ideal paper has subtle seasonings that release upon chewing.

Some artificial flavors worked well (see worm comments later in this lesson), and others were epic failures (e.g., the McDonald's French Fry fragrance). Our panel of tasters found some surprise winners in this category.

Tearability

Papers that score highest on this metric tear unevenly rather than in strips, so your dog can shred them into tiny, jagged pieces. Satisfyingly small pieces that make a large pile are fun to clean up—for humans, that is. They like monotonous games like crosswords, jigsaw puzzles, and 52-card pickup; we're happy to oblige.

Most heavy-weight commercial wrapping papers tear into strips, whereas lightweight papers usually tear unevenly and score higher. Our team found several bargain papers that ranked high on this metric.

Texture

Our panel found textured papers more of a distraction than an advantage. However, they liked soft papers that melted on the tongue to produce surprising and subtle texture changes and a tangy bite.

Crinkle Quality

Crinkle is essential to a dog's unwrapping experience, and here again, we found several bargains that crinkled better than expensive name brands. In our esteemed panel's opinion, foil-backed papers tear too straight and have too little crinkle—a victim of over-engineering. Sometimes, less is more.

Conclusion

Our canine experts reviewed hundreds of wrapping alternatives to give dogs the best unwrapping experience. We found wrapping papers that can meet any budget, including some that will evoke memories of a sun-dried worm on a cool autumn day before it gets baked through—crispy on the outside, yet juicy in the middle.

Excuse me, I have to go. Dinner is calling. Literally, it's calling me.

Job Opportunity: Assistant Editor

Are you looking for an exciting career in canine publishing? We have an opening for an assistant editor with skills in chewing, typing, and butt-sniffing. Please send us an email with your breed and typing speed, and cite previous canine publications or doggie literary awards. We are an AEEO (Almost Equal Employment Opportunist)—poodles need not apply.

Lesson 36: The Consequences of Unwrapping Someone Else's Present

Always make sure you fully consume the evidence

In *The Joys of Unwrapping Gifts,* I extolled the virtues of chewing wrapping paper. In this lesson, I'll share a story of a present unwrapping gone bad.

On this occasion, I spied a present left in a bag on the floor, nicely wrapped and snuggled among pink tissue paper. I rarely find a present left unattended at my level, as I am what's known as "vertically challenged." Okay, I heard that snigger and know all the jokes already. Keep it to yourself.

Usually, I work around my height issues because I'm a good climber, but there was no need that day. There it was, sitting on the floor next to Mommy's desk, taunting me.

"Keke," it said. "Show us your true grit. Are you a dog or a kitty?"

As you can see, I had no choice. I started with the tissues, but after scattering the pieces about the floor, the only thing left in the bag was the present.

It wore a pink ribbon over its brown wrapping paper. It called to me, asking me to reveal its secrets. The aroma was strawberry with hidden undertones of forbidden fruit.

It was lighter than expected, and I held it with my paws. Thanks to my broad experience untying Daddy's shoelaces, I quickly removed the ribbon and bow.

Next, I tugged at the brown wrappings. Sometimes, you can find yourself rushed by an army of onlookers. But when you are alone, it can be a relief to savor the process and enjoy the complex flavors, fragrances, and textures.

I carefully tore the paper into tiny shreds, making a pleasing little pile, like the type I make in my daily wanderings in the grass.

The contents were soft and squishy but encased in strong plastic wrap with a crisp cellophane crinkle. This was going to be good.

After several attempts, I broke through the cellophane with my teeth, revealing a pink marshmallow filling. The pungent strawberry flavor erupted, like biting into a starburst candy.

I was a shark smelling blood, tearing frantically at the crisp plastic. My adversary put up a good fight but was no match for my razor-sharp fangs.

The cellophane covering was too tough to shred, but I quickly licked it clean.

I had no sense of time. I may have laid there picking through the bones of my quarry for a minute or an hour. It didn't matter. Such are the simple pleasures of complete fulfillment.

At some point, my humans returned from their activities. I decided to dissociate myself from the incriminating evidence on the floor. A distraction would help, too, so I trotted to the front door, the picture of innocence as I patiently waited to be let out.

As Mommy bent to attach the leash to my harness, two things happened. The first was a well-tuned guttural eruption as my stomach expressed its satisfaction with the recently consumed pink sweet. In other words, I burped.

The second was a nose sniff.

My ears are well attuned to the sound of a sniffing nose because it usually means somebody is checking me out, but the nose's owner is generally of the four-legged variety, not two.

Humans' olfactory senses are underdeveloped, so I rarely consider that they might use my scent against me. But some humans are enormously fond of certain odors and can recognize them from a distance. Even eons of negative evolution have not worked their magic on certain scents like a barbecued steak or a favorite candy, and she seemed to have detected such a rare fragrance.

"Keke, what's that smell?"

Next, she picked me up to examine me more closely. I looked away, but not quickly enough.

"What's that pink stuff on your nose and mouth?"

When caught red-handed (or pink-mouthed), the best thing is to feign ignorance, which comes second nature to me. She sniffed more closely at the damning evidence, then asked me straight out: "Did you get into that present by my desk?"

Luckily, dogs are not expected to answer such questions, so there was no need to plead the Fifth.

For those of you who enjoy crime shows like *Law and Order*, let me tell you their portrayals are not realistic. There is no time spent examining evidence, taking fingerprints or DNA samples, searching for corroborating witnesses, or presenting said evidence before a judge before returning a verdict and announcing sentencing. Nor are there opportunities for appeal.

The judge heard the case, condemned the perpetrator, and meted out punishment, all in about ten seconds. Fortunately, as this was a first offense, the punishment consisted primarily of a lecture about the dangers of consuming unknown substances and the possible suffocation of said consumer should she swallow the plastic wrapping.

I could have countered with my own lecture on the importance of keeping dangerous substances out of reach of children or innocent puppies, but this didn't seem the right time.

Then, she launched into a diatribe on other subjects. I wasn't listening because I still had a little gob of strawberry marshmallow on my lip and needed to lick it all off before anyone tried to wipe it with a damp towel— which, in fact, happened only seconds later.

It's important to learn from one's mistakes to avoid repeating them. Here, the error was in failing to cover my tracks, which resulted in losing my case before it began. Always make sure you fully consume the evidence.

The outcome of this story is that I got off with only a lecture about the dangers of dabbling in someone else's belongings. Of course, I might not be so lucky on my second offense, but how will I know if I don't try?

Lesson 37: A Dog's Unconditional Love

On the nuances of love & keeping up with the Wests

Learning to love your human requires patience, understanding, and a tolerance for bad breath and strange body odors, especially after a late night of partying. But it also has excellent benefits: belly rubs, someone to scratch those areas you can't reach, and that sweet-n-salty taste of Black Cherry Merlot hand cream mixed with a light sweat residue. It's like a salted caramel yogurt-covered granola bar, only better.

Apart from licking, loving your humans requires snuggling and tissues. Lots of tissues—not for crying or blowing your nose, but for shredding. Earlier, I wrote about the joys of shredding tissues and the lovely little pile of tissue detritus that someone will eventually clean up. (Hint: it won't be me.) Tissues also sometimes come with a hidden salty flavor burst.

My humans are good about picking up the tissue pieces without complaint because they enjoy seeing me rip into the tissue almost as much as I enjoy doing it. Are they living vicariously, or are they just relieved that my mischief is momentarily confined to something they can see and monitor and won't be expensive to replace?

I like to show my love for my humans, even when they feed me Brussels Sprouts or hog the blanket and pillow. It's okay. We all have our moments of selfishness sometimes. Nobody's perfect.

If you're lucky enough to have little humans in your house, they can be even more fun than the big ones. When a child plays, you get their undivided attention. There are no smartphones to check, no "responsibilities" to distract them, no blogs or podcasts to post. They give you pure, uninterrupted love. And mealtimes with children can be a goldmine of dropped food and delicious seconds on the face, hands, and whatever else you can reach.

If I'm not too busy picking up dropped table scraps during mealtimes, I like to show my love by chewing on shoelaces. During playtime, I let them win occasionally. When they return home, I wag my tail so fast they think it's a whirling helicopter propeller about to take off. At bedtime, I curl up next to them and only whimper a little when they banish me to the penal colony. And on special occasions, I unwrap the presents and shred all the paper until it covers the floor like so many ant hills.

I love my Mommy and Daddy just as they are, and they love me. And that's even better than all the wrapping paper at North West's birthday.

I can't wait for my first Christmas. I'm told our house might come close to North's.

Lesson 38: Halloween Is Coming. Is Your Dog Equipped to Defend Your House Against Ruthless Invaders?

Five tips for picking canine costumes

![Dog wearing an Iron Man costume]

Halloween is coming, and hordes of monsters, zombies, soldiers, and other evil beasts will soon invade your house. They will come to your door demanding treats under threat of performing tricks on your household.

How can you defend your home against such threats? How can you arm yourself with the tools necessary to counter a full-scale home invasion?

For this article, I reviewed incoming threats and tested available defenses to provide this invaluable guide to protecting your homestead against the annual October invasion.

Following are five essential tips for picking your canine Halloween wardrobe that will arm you to the teeth and avoid the shame of a lame ensemble.

1. Show authority

We dogs have always had a monumental responsibility to protect our homes from invaders. Our job is to stop potential intruders before they ever reach the house through a combination of intimidation, threats, and bribery. We must command respect, and for this, our appearance should project an image of authority. Good examples are police officers, soldiers, superheroes, and skilled negotiators. Can you imagine the look on an intruder's face when Iron Man appears at the door on jet-powered roller skates?

2. Project power

Suppose you secured an Iron Man costume. Wouldn't it be cool to hold a repulsor ray in one paw and the family cat in another? You want to throw the kitty at your visitor (because—duh—what else would you do with it?) and then blast the cat with your repulsor ray to ensure it never returns.

That will make the intruder (and the cat) think twice, but if they come back, be ready with a

Ghostbusters green slime machine. Oh boy, that cat will be history after a good slime attack, don't you think?

3. Instill fear

Your aim is to induce fear in the hearts of your subjects. Fear of those growling fangs, those razor-sharp nails, and a tongue that will lick them to death if they renege on their promise to play "fetch" with your favorite squeaky toy.

4. Display a vicious streak a mile wide

It's important to show your adversary that you are ruthless and unpredictable. Keep them guessing whether that pink tongue will lick them or give them a harsh raspberry.

5. Be open to negotiations

Let's face it: a dog requires support and respect from the humans in the household. If your humans interrupt your vicious barks with a warning like, "Keke, hush!" what can you do? How can you drive off zombies if your bark is perceived to lack bite?

In the end, if all the above techniques fail, you may be forced to reach an agreement with these terrorists. You need to be a tough negotiator. I'm thinking of Denzel Washington in *Inside Man*. Demand only the highest quality puppy treats, like "Chicken Chips" or "Pupperonis." Don't be bought off with second-rate dog bones.

If all else fails, "Run away!"

And don't forget to protect your tail by tucking it between your legs.

Lesson 39: Vampires and Other Murderous Monsters on the Loose

Murder, Mystery, and Mouse Droppings

It was a restless night. The night before, we had gone to the village square to join the Halloween festivities, and I had worn my ghost costume. I was a scary apparition but hardly the invincible Iron Man I'd hoped for. There were many more frightening creatures out there.

Zombies that looked like they had just stepped from the grave writhed on the ground to the tune of "Thriller." Frankenstein, his green head bobbing in time to the music, roared an evil laugh when he saw me. To my right, vampires with bloodied shirts sat at a table, drinking deeply from smoking mugs. They spoke in hushed tones, one eyeing me and grinning, his white fangs glistening in the moonlight.

That night, I dreamed of those fangs dripping with fresh blood, a dark red tongue darting about an evil, smiling mouth.

In the morning, I awoke to an unfamiliar odor in the house: a fetid stench of decay mixed with a dash of evil omen. I searched for the source of the smell, finally finding a furry brown lump on the floor by the living room bar. It had the rancid smell of decaying flesh.

"Mousey!" I called, hoping my friend could identify the corpse.

"Eeeek!" he exclaimed as he arrived by my side. "It's a dead mouse."

"Wonder where it came from."

Mousey turned to me, eyes bulging. "It was murdered in cold blood!"

I inched closer despite the stench. I wondered aloud how he could tell it was murder.

"Look at the teeth marks," he said, pointing to a round hole in the mouse's neck and another about an inch away near the front leg.

"But who would do such a thing?"

Mousey narrowed his eyes as his gaze met mine. "There's only one thing that would kill a defenseless mouse for fun. It's that cat."

I had seen little of the cat since we'd agreed to a truce, but I knew it was still living under my roof. My brave alter-ego, Dragontooth, had chased the cat away, only to have my humans welcome the "kitty" back.

Mousey had convinced me cats were cruel and evil, but the humans had overridden me. The cat and I finally agreed to an arrangement: It would have the back bedroom, and I would have the rest of the house.

I immediately went to the beast's lair to confront my nemesis. Mousey stayed behind out of fear for his life.

I found the cat on its favorite window ledge, its brown, black, and yellow striped body poking out from behind the blinds.

"Hey, furball!" I called. "Why'd you kill the mouse in the living room?"

The cat blinked. "The name's Zoey," she said. "And you're a fine one to call names, being a furball yourself."

"I'm a hair dog," I said, turning my head to show off my silky mane. "I don't have fur."

Zoey responded with a cough and a choking sound.

"Are you okay?" I asked.

"Hairball," she said, chuckling.

I ignored the taunt. "So, why'd you kill the mouse?"

She looked down from her shelf and narrowed her eyes. "I haven't touched any mice in this house."

"So you deny knowing anything about it?"

"Oh, I got a good whiff of it. Anyone with half a nostril could detect the dead body for the past two days. But it was not my concern."

Mousey was the first to speak as we re-examined the dead rodent. "So, did you wring a confession out of that frosty feline?"

Ignoring his question, I pointed at the fang holes in the corpse. "Zoey's snout is about the same size as mine."

"You mean the cat? Are you on a first-name basis now?"

"Yes, her name is Zoey. And her fangs wouldn't be much farther apart than mine. But the distance between these holes is twice that of my fangs."

"What's the difference?" Mousey said. "Nothing else could have killed it."

Looking over my shoulder, Mousey suggested that the cat had gotten the mouse with just one fang, then moved her mouth over and made the second puncture. "Maybe with the same fang," he added.

"Hmmm," I said. "Maybe."

This time, I convinced Mousey to join me in confronting Zoey. "Dragontooth will protect you," I promised. Mousey knew what Dragontooth was capable of, having been caught by my alter-ego once before.

As we entered the back bedroom, the cat stopped licking her paws. "Back again so soon?"

"Zoey," I said. "Could you please show us your teeth?"

"I'd rather not," the cat replied, rubbing its head against the window corner.

"Why not? Do you have something to hide?"

"You're in my part of the house again," Zoey warned. "And you're barking up my tree."

I pointed out that if she killed the mouse, she was in my section of the house.

"I already told you I didn't kill it." She resumed her grooming.

"Listen," I said. "You had motive—it's in the genes for cats to track and kill mice. And you had opportunity while everyone was asleep in the house. I'm trying to determine if you had the means. We can clear this up quickly if you show us your teeth."

Zoey yawned, a vast, gaping yawn that revealed an empty mouth.

Mousey gasped, and I said, "You have no teeth!"

"I have a few molars in the back," the cat said. "Are we done now?"

"Yes, and I'm sorry we bothered you."

Mousey stared at me. "So that's it? You're giving up because it has no teeth?"

"Not just yet."

Later that day, I called Mousey back to the crime scene.

"Not again," the mouse complained.

"Look at this."

Mousey looked and shrugged. "Mouse droppings. So what?"

"Are they yours?"

Mousey sniffed the pellets and shook his head.

"The presence of droppings next to the body tells me the mouse lay here, perhaps for a day or more before it died."

"Maybe it slept here," Mousey suggested.

"I don't think so," I said. "This is not a good hiding place."

"What difference does it make? Who else would murder a mouse in cold blood except a killer cat?"

I pointed to the fang holes. "And what made these holes? Zoey doesn't have teeth."

"Maybe she wore fake teeth, like the vampire teeth humans put in their mouths for Halloween."

"You mean like these?" I asked, producing a pair of white plastic teeth with fangs. I held it against the dead mouse, and the fang holes aligned perfectly.

"Exactly!" exclaimed Mousey.

"And what were these plastic teeth doing behind your bed?"

The mouse squirmed and avoided my eyes. "Maybe someone put them there?"

"Maybe that someone was you?"

Mousey sniffed. "Okay, I found the mouse dead of natural causes. I discovered those vampire teeth and made the fang holes, so you'd think the cat killed it."

"But why would you do that? What did Zoey do to you?"

"It's a cat! It's only a matter of time before it hunts mice again."

"Mousey," I said. "Not everyone is what they appear to be. Some cats might be nice."

Mousey apologized for lying, but I said it was Zoey who deserved his apology. "And try to get to know her," I suggested. "Don't judge a creature by its droppings."

"Eeeeek!"

"Well, you don't have to get all melodramatic about it," I said. I turned to look at Mousey. He was staring at the window, mouth frozen in a scream.

Lesson 40: I Love the Fall

A dog's view on the change of seasons

I love the fall. Everything changes. The smells, the lights, the colors, the temperatures, even the time. I have a human who says, "Oh yes, I get to sleep an extra hour." But I have a puppy bladder that says, "Oh no, don't even think about it."

I love the walks on those cool, clear mornings. And the days are getting shorter, making it harder for humans to see things on evening walks. Dogs are not as reliant on sight, so it doesn't matter as much to us. We can still sniff the fragrances and discover changing animal patterns. And we can pick up things in our mouths that humans won't see. But I'm getting ahead of myself—more on that later.

The smells of fall are very different from summer. Whereas flowers, fruits, and freshly cut grass dominate the bouquets carried on a summer breeze, autumn winds transport earthy smells as trees and bushes shed their leaves. Then the leaves fall and decay on the ground.

Autumn scents are less intense—more subtle—allowing the air currents to carry distant aromas, unmasked by nearby smells. There is a farm a half mile from our house, and in the summer I can hear the crowing of roosters, the mooing of cows, and the braying of donkeys. But it's only in the fall that I can smell the animals themselves, as their scents carry longer distances on the winds.

Speaking of animals, strange birds occupy the sky. Big honkers travel in "V" formations, and smaller birds cackle and chirp as their flocks form erratic patterns across the sky.

The flowers are gone. Trees and bushes cling to their last leaves until a stiff breeze tears them loose. Oh, look, there goes one now—better chase it!

The other thing I love about the fall is the football season.

I am Haason Reddick, linebacker for the Philadelphia Eagles, and the Dallas Cowboys are at fourth and goal. I spring through the Dallas defenses to sack the quarterback and seize the dead leaf—I mean football—from his hands. Oh no, three more footballs are skittering across the field. Wait, how many are there?

The best thing about catching leaves is their noisy crackle when I bite into them. Crunch, crunch. The taste is woody and utterly different from green leaves—which are delicious, too, but in a caterpillar-ish way.

When the leaves bury themselves in the grass or pile up in a corner, they decay. I like to stick my nose deep in the grass and breathe in the scents. Decaying leaves smell like a peat bog with new fungi growing. Old poop smells like, well, old poop.

And then there are the acorns that fall on the ground. They roll and fit nicely in my mouth—sometimes, I carry one for an entire walk. That is, until we get home, and Daddy tells me to drop it before we go inside. But it's okay—what he doesn't know won't hurt him. I have five more in my mouth.

Lesson 41: Who is the Alpha Dog in the House?

Training your vacation landlords

Recently, I spent a week living with John and Diane, friends of my humans who abandoned me for a "vacation." Why anyone would want a vacation without their primary source of entertainment, puppy licks, and tissue pulp, is beyond me. But off they went, and behind I stayed.

John and Diane welcomed me into their home and told me I could pee and poop anywhere I liked but could only sleep on the pee pads or outside. Or maybe I got those mixed up a little.

There were many new places to explore near their house, which backed onto a small lake populated by play toys called "ducks." Ducks are odd creatures that have only two legs (except for one that hopped on a single leg), making them easy marks for the vastly superior, sleek four-legged design of yours truly. The one advantage nature gave them is wings. Still, unlike birds, they need a runway and several seconds of taxiing before they can lift off. Left to my own devices, I calculated I could intercept 90% of them before they became airborne, even with a thirty-foot lead.

Unfortunately, their lead was considerably longer owing to the escape plan they had worked out with my captors, which included a harness and leash much shorter than thirty feet.

A little frustrating, to say the leashed.

The lake water initially appeared flat and undisturbed. Being a keen observer, I uncovered two secrets of that small body of water. One was the fish that lived in it, occasionally breaking the surface as they chased, or were chased by, other creatures of the black lagoon. I longed to swim with these scaly toys and discover their fellow inhabitants, but the second secret stopped me.

The second secret was a slow-moving, scaly rock that floated along the water's surface and occasionally disappeared beneath. It also beckoned to me, but prudence intervened and cautioned me to keep my distance. Or maybe her name was Diane. In any case, she was the holder of the leash, as well as the puppy treats, so her preferences were worth considering.

Oh, and the third secret is that I can't swim. Or at least, my first attempt went over like a lead bathosphere. (See my lesson, "Conclusion of Keke's Vacation at the Beach.")

John and Diane were charming hosts, and we had fun inventing new games. John uses a long "walking stick," something like the lamppost Gene Kelly danced around in "Singin' In The Rain," with the added challenge that it moves as he walks. He was no Cyd Charrise, but did his best to keep up.

My hosts were wonderful, loving people happy to share their home with me. Maybe "happy" was not the initial reaction, but I grew on them like a leech. They learned to love me, and the feelings were mutual. Their ankles were particularly tasty after a shower.

Unfortunately, they lacked training in the finer points of living with a puppy. But, I have always enjoyed a challenge and attacked their education with my usual verve.

I've written extensively in this blog about my attempts to teach humans the not-so-subtle art of House Training for Puppies. You may want to read Part 1 of House Training for Puppies: A Little Dab'll Do Ya and Part 2 of House Training for Puppies, found elsewhere in this book. (Future landlords, take note, and please review these two lessons before my arrival. It will save a great deal of confusion.)

At one point, after I peed on the floor to demonstrate proper housetraining techniques, Diane picked me up and said, "I am the alpha dog in this house! Do you understand?" Clearly, she was confused about the pecking order, not to mention the instructional aids I needed to employ.

Despite the lapse in proper educational materials, this couple was ultimately trainable, albeit with more stress than necessary. I'm sure they'll get better next time.

Lesson 42: I Love Those Crazy Squirrels (Even if They're Not So Nuts About Me)

Three things you probably never knew about squirrels

Squirrels are great fun to chase any time of the year, but I see them most in the fall when they're busy gathering and storing food for winter. Their coats are lighter this time of year, their bodies turning silver-grey and their faces changing from buffy-brown to white. I discussed in an earlier lesson why I love the fall. In this post, I'll talk about why I love squirrels (especially in the fall), and you'll learn three things you probably didn't know about them.

1. Did you know squirrels have four toes on their front feet but five on their back?

At first glance, they look like human hands. Their front paws have four long digits plus a short, stubby thumb, but five long digits on the back paws.

Claws allow them to grasp tiny bumps in a tree's bark and scale a massive trunk, yet the same toothpick-sized digits can also wrap around a twig and allow climbing the highest branches. And they can hold a nut in a single paw.

They're equally adept at hopping or running on the ground, as the situation requires. And, of course, those amazing paws can climb trees, hold nuts, and play the intro to *Rhapsody in Blue* on the clarinet.

2. Did you know squirrels' back legs are double-jointed?

Think about it. Humans can climb a tree, but did you ever consider *climbing down head-first*? Those crazy squirrels can do it. They climb up a tree trunk using hook-like claws to grasp tiny bumps in the bark. They climb down the same way, but it wouldn't work if the claws were all facing forward. Instead, they turn their back paws around 180 degrees. This trick allows them to hang onto a tree trunk upside-down or climb down head-first.

People call my humans "tree huggers," but they have nothing on squirrels!

I saw a squirrel on the ground during my last walk. My friend Flash, a pit bull-labrador mix, was coming in the opposite direction and spied the squirrel from a distance. Little Nutty's pea-sized ears perked up, and his dark black eyes bulged as he watched Flash. He seemed focused on the larger dog, so I went into a pouncing crouch, creeping along the ground like a lioness stalking her prey. I wanted to signal Flash to stay quiet so we could corner the squirrel between us, and for a moment, we were close. The squirrel sat up, mouth moving noiselessly, tail twitching nervously.

Until my human saw Flash's human and yelled, "Hi, Joe!"

The squirrel leaped nearly ten feet to a nearby oak tree before I could whisper, "Hush!"

Once on the tree trunk, the squirrel climbed fifteen feet to the first branch. There he sat, chattering, scolding us for interrupting his valuable nut-gathering time. His cheeks bulged larger than his eyes, and I wondered how he could scold without dropping the cache of food from his jowls.

Speaking of nuts, training your human to sneak up on something can be very frustrating. Thousands of years of stalking hamburger patties in an air-conditioned grocery store have dulled their senses and minds.

But back to my story. I walked beneath the oak tree, watching the squirrel climb higher, jumping branch to branch like Tarzan. I wished I could follow.

As he neared the uppermost branches, his hind paws grabbed the tree, and he hung upside down, still clicking his mouth and twitching his tail, looking directly at me. Flash had moved on.

The squirrel took an acorn from his mouth, and I watched as it fell from his forepaw and bounced to the ground.

Hey, mister, you dropped one. Let me get it for you.

Let me see, I think it was this... ouch! That landed on my butt. Ouch! That one landed on my head! Hey, that was no accident.

Come down here, you nut job, and I'll show you some of MY toys. Do you know how to play *Mousetrap*? How about *Operation*?

3. A squirrel hides behind its own tail

Did you know the word "Squirrel" comes from the Greek for "Shadow Tail"? That's because squirrels use their long, bushy tails to cast a shadow, obscuring their presence from predators. Pretty neat, huh?

And I've learned something else about squirrels in the fall: they're bulking up. Which means they're slowing down. Which just might give me a better chance at catching one.

I'm coming for you, mein Freund!

Lesson 43: Sailors, Scoundrels, and Pirates on the Sea

Seize the helm and change tack

Every sailor knows it's bad luck to start a voyage on a Friday. Or really, any day that ends in a 'Y,' but what did I know? It was my first time on a sailboat.

I had my new life jacket on, pink with white polka dots. It was a little girly for a formidable pirate like myself, but it would have to do. A lengthy ocean crossing was no place for fashionistas—not when I was about to confront my deepest fears.

Like, did anyone remember to pack lunch?

But that day, I was Jack Sparrow, about to change tack and sneak aboard the Black Pearl, now under the command of the backstabbing Hector Barbossa. A daytime moon hung like a stolen pearl in the sky, and rustling breezes whispered tales of mutiny, treachery, and fresh droppings on the poop deck.

I made no sound as I navigated the shadows of my pride and joy, which now sailed under a black flag of betrayal. I had come to reclaim what was rightfully mine. My beloved Pearl had slipped through my paws like a rogue leaf on a fall day, but today would be my day for revenge.

First, I had to rescue my dear Elizabeth, trapped in the brig. She was a damsel in distress, waiting for a hairier and cuter pirate than Barbossa to save her from her confinement.

The once-hallowed planks groaned as I slipped below decks.

Approaching the brig, I grasped the hilt of my trusty cutlass. The guard was a disheveled scallywag and snored louder than a drunken sailor in a rum-soaked tavern. With one swift motion, he found himself face-first on the hard, unforgiving floor. The Sparrow had overcome him with barely a peep.

I found the key and unlocked the brig door, revealing Elizabeth's delicate figure huddled in the corner. Her eyes widened upon seeing me, and she looked at me with a mixture of relief and surprise. "Jack?" she whispered.

"In the flesh, love," I replied, extending a paw to help her. "Now, if you'll grab my leash, there's a certain matter of reclaiming my ship and dealing with a mutinous scoundrel."

Together, we tiptoed the shadowed corridors of the Pearl. We reached the main deck to see Hector barking orders to his crew, the treacherous wretches scurrying about like squirrels in a ship full of nuts.

"Barbossa!" I called. The captain turned, a wicked smirk playing on his lips.

"Jack Sparrow, alive and well, I see. I thought you met your end in the Chihuahua Teddy's embrace."

"A minor inconvenience, my dear Hector," I replied as I swaggered onto the deck with Elizabeth at my side. "And now, I've come to reclaim what's rightfully mine."

The battle was a chaotic symphony of clashing swords and punishing licks. Elizabeth proved her mettle, fighting alongside me with a determination rivaling the fiercest dog walkers. Barbossa's crew faltered beneath the combined might of our cunning and our poop launchers.

Ultimately, it came down to a duel between Barbossa and me. Our blades danced in the sunlight, the clash of steel echoing across the silent sea. With a swift parry and a well-timed tongue-lashing, I disarmed Barbossa, leaving him deflated and defeated.

"Now, Hector," I said, smiling, "I believe it's time for you to take an extended vacation to Isla de Muerta."

As the crew surrendered and the Black Pearl returned to her rightful captain, I couldn't help but feel the familiar embrace of the ocean breezes, the fall of acorns, and the call of adventure. It was my turn to growl orders at the crew.

"Hoist the Jolly Roger! Let's whip these scurvy scallywags into shape or keelhaul the lot of 'em!"

With Elizabeth at my side, the horizon stretched before us like a canvas of endless possibilities. At least as far as Lake Harris would take us.

Lesson 44: What's In Your Stomach?

A dog's view on human eating

Humans worry a lot about what they eat and drink. They fuss over saturated fats, trans fats, sodium, and cholesterol. They fret if they're consuming too much sugar and worry if they're drinking artificial sweeteners.

Don't eat red meats, and avoid chicken because it's filled with hormones and antibiotics. Stay away from farm-raised fish, but eat the wild-caught ones and you'll die from mercury poisoning.

And whatever you do, don't get a conscience, or you'll never eat anything that ever moved under its own power because their living conditions are deplorable.

And for God's sake, stay away from carbs or dessert. You've got to look like a supermodel in those form-fitting clothes, or people will think you're not taking care of yourself. Which, in fact, you're not, as you'll see if you read on.

Historically, humans have turned to diets to save themselves from this pressure.

A brief history of dieting

Unlike dogs, humans have practiced the art of dieting since ancient Greek times. Hippocrates recommended fat people follow a strict daily menu, increase their exercise, and vomit.

However, he did not need to follow his own advice since he was the founder of the ancient Greek political party, the Hippocrats.

The first liquid diet dates to the eleventh century when William the Conqueror grew so fat that he couldn't mount his horse. Giving up food, he consumed only alcohol—a real man's liquid diet. When he finally got on his horse again, the saddle horn caught in his gut, and he died of an infection.

Alas, he was still so fat that he couldn't fit in his coffin.

The first diet book was written in 1558 by Italian Luigi Cornaro. It advised readers to limit their daily intake to 12 ounces of food and 14 ounces of wine.

Like William, he thought you wouldn't notice you were starving if you drank enough alcohol.

In the nineteenth century, Lord Byron emerged as the first "diet influencer," a social media star ahead of his time owing to his tales of binging and starving and his trendy "vinegar diet." It was so popular that some women in the 1800s died from drinking pints of vinegar. Fortunately, no one had invented bleach at that time.

As you can see, diets have never worked out well for either humans or pets.

What to do? How can you save your humans from themselves?

Humans literally worry themselves to death over this stuff. Look at the facts: chronic stress causes cancer. And cancer is the second most common cause of death in the United States.

Look, I'm no doctor; I'm not even a veterinarian. But speaking from a dog's perspective, let me give you humans some advice:

Eat like a dog.

If it tastes good, devour it. Don't wait to read the labels; just peel them off. Or don't peel them off—you might find you like them too. It gives your meal an extra crunch, like chewing through a pile of wrapping paper. For more on this topic, see my lesson on The Joys of Unwrapping Gifts.

You'll lead happier, stress-free, longer lives. My recommendation: Check out Cesar Filet Mignon Flavor. Or, for the heartier appetite, try Alpo Prime Cuts. You might like them.

From what I've seen, eating a diet of kale, tofu, and quinoa can lead you to an obsessive-compulsive disorder that can increase worry and decrease friendships: buying watches that count calories and steps, fanatical dieting, and an impulse to tell everyone around you how they're doing everything wrong.

Telling your kids, "No dessert until you finish all your vegetables," will never win you "Mom of the Year" glories.

If you choose to eat that hot fudge brownie sundae with whipped cream and a cherry on top, just shut up about it and work it off by playing with a cute puppy. Or take her for a long walk.

Because human eating habits are self-mutilation, a form of self-imposed capital punishment called cancer. And since cancer is the number two killer, I call it "Capital Two."

And Capital Two wants to know:

What's in YOUR stomach?

Lesson 45: Thanksgiving With the Twins

On humor, rubber chickens, and thankfulness

Thanksgiving brings a houseful of guests, including three young boys.

Oh boy, I love kids!

Liam, the older one, is a little reserved, but the twin five-year-olds, Connor and Logan, are ready to rumble like a South African rugby team. My kind of peeps.

The first thing the twins notice is the large orange button on the floor by the front door. It's there for me to push when I need to go out, and when depressed, a recorded voice says, "Pee-pee!"

Connor steps on the button.

"Pee-pee!"

The boys giggle. Logan pushes it.

"Pee-pee!"

More giggling. It's Liam's turn.

"Pee-pee!"

Peals of laughter.

It's an inside joke, and I am on the outside.

The adults turn on the television, and for the moment, the boys settle in to watch the Thanksgiving Day parade. Grogu, Scrat, and Pikachu float overhead like clouds from another world while dancers below undulate in waves like a field of yellow poppies. Grogu's hovering pram ball veers side to side like a leaf blowing in the wind, and Goku from Dragon Ball appears to be having a bad hair day—kind of like I look after playing "Find the Puppy" under the blankets.

After the parade, we go to the lake to feed the turtles and fishies. Not too many fish by the docks today, but there are three or four giant turtles. The boys heave fistfuls of food at the water, the dock, and innocent bystanders.

Hey, make them work for it: no free treats around here!

I'll teach those turtles to fetch.

I pick up some misfires. Pa-tooey! It tastes like overripe avocados compressed into little brown cardboard nuggets. I'll leave this lesson to the kids.

Once the boys have exhausted both the supplies and the turtles, we go home. Tantalizing aromas fill the house. I salivate over the smell of oven-roasted turkey stuffed with sausage-pecan stuffing, a roast seasoned with garlic and rosemary, and onion potatoes.

What do you mean, it's not ready to eat yet? Just put it down here, and I'll keep an eye on it for you.

It's time to play "Pin the hat on the turkey." One by one, the boys are blindfolded and spun around.

Hey, who are you calling a turkey? Unstick that hat from my head!

With no warning, little rubber chickens are suddenly flying across the room. There must be four hundred, and the boys are throwing them everywhere. They stick to the walls, the ceiling, and Daddy's head. Some of them fall off, but others cling. Daddy takes the chicken off his head, only to have another one stick there a moment later.

I have to admit, that was funny.

A minute later, I hear, "Pee-pee!"

Someone moved the button, and now the sound is coming from the living room.

Hey, Momma, I think those boys need a potty break. Why don't you take them out?

Football games are on T.V. Who's playing?

The twins are! It's a different kind of "football," but more to my liking. Connor starts the kick-off with my purple soccer ball.

I am Megan Rapinoe, facing down the famous Swedish soccer duo in the deciding match of the Women's World Cup. Connor passes to Logan, but I'm too fast for them. With a menacing growl, I steal the ball, fake left, then drive right. I'm within one yard of the goal when a foot collides with my mouth. Ughhh. Timeout called.

But this rugged American winger is on her feet before the timeout is up. Emitting a loud bark, I hit the ball with my nose, sending it flying past the surprised Swedes to score the game's first goal.

Logan has the ball. But Connor tosses my dragon toy onto the field. He's trying to bait me, but I'll show him how I deal with this illegal maneuver. I spring on the surprised dragon, which erupts with a spout of flame and a loud c-r-u-n-ch! The field is totally under my control now.

But wait, Logan dribbles past me and punts an easy goal. I can't believe I fell for that.

Then again, I still have the dragon, and Connor wants it. He'll have to pry it from my cold, dead mouth.

R-r-r-i-p! How did he get that dragon away so fast?

I'll show him. I get my mousey toy.

Wait, was that my squeaky eel that Connor just threw past my head? Grrr-owl.

I'll get it back. What's Lamb Chop doing on the field? Hey, you leave her out of this!

Was that a rubber chicken that hit my butt? And my head? And my side? I pick up a rubber chicken in my mouth, climb to the back of the couch where Logan is hiding, drop the chicken on him, and run away.

"Hey!" I hear from behind the couch...

* * *

Thanksgiving Dinner is finally served. Everyone sits at the dining room table, and Liam asks us all to say what we're thankful for.

I'm thankful for my Lamb Chop stuffie and my squeaky mouse. I'm grateful for Mommy and Daddy, who love me, steal the blankets at night, and wake me up at 3 AM with their snoring. I'll share my bed with them anyway.

And I'm thankful for Liam and the dynamic duo of human tornadoes who have endless giggles, love to throw my toys and shoot rubber chickens across the house.

Yawn. I'll close my eyes for a minute while I wait for leftovers.

I wake up. I'm in bed, next to Mommy and Daddy. The morning sun is peeking through the blinds.

I race down the stairs and into the living room.

Connor? Logan?

The house is silent, and the living room is empty. I check the guest bedroom. It's unoccupied. I run to the front door, and the orange button has returned to its usual spot. I step on it.

"Pee-pee!"

Not a sound in the house.

Hee-hee. I press it again.

"Pee-pee!"

This is silly. I hear Daddy getting out of bed, but I can't resist.

"Pee-pee!"

"Okay, Keke, I heard you the first time. I'm coming!"

Ha-ha-ha!

What a great Thanksgiving. When will the boys be back?

Lesson 46: Naughty or Nice List

What skeletons are in your closet?

![Person wearing a hooded jacket and skull mask]

"So let me get this straight," I said to Mousey. "Santa has a nice list and a naughty list. If I'm on his nice list, I get lots of presents for Christmas. But if I'm on the naughty list, I get nothing?"

"Well, you *might* get a lump of coal," said the little mouse, his brow knitted.

I gulped hard, thinking about all the times I'd been bad. "Do you think Daddy told him about the time I purposely peed on the floor after he forgot to give me a treat?"

"He doesn't have to. Santa sees you when you're sleeping and when you're awake." The mouse was remarkably calm as he delivered this bombshell. "And don't forget the incident with the pink candy," he added.

I had forgotten all about the candy I had stolen from Mommy and eaten. "So some creepy old guy I've never seen has been watching me twenty-four-seven?"

"Yup."

"Why is this the first I'm hearing about this?"

I exclaimed, breaking into a sweat. "I'm just a little puppy. I never heard of this naughty list before!"

Mousey considered my outburst. "Maybe we should talk to Zoey. She's been around a lot longer than I have."

I couldn't believe the mouse was suggesting talking to her proclaimed worst enemy, but it seemed like a good idea.

We cautiously approached the cat's lair, not wanting to disturb her afternoon nap. But as we entered the back bedroom, we found the giant tabby perched on her favorite windowsill, her tail flicking carelessly as she watched us approach.

"Hey, Zoey," I called. "Have you heard about Santa and his naughty list?"

"Mmmm," the cat purred, rubbing her chin against the window. "And you two are worried about your misdeeds?" She fixed a stern gaze on Mousey as she said, "Like the time you tried to frame me for murder?"

The mouse sucked in a deep breath.

"I've been naughty too," I said, trying to divert the conversation. Staring at the floor, I gave an accounting of my misadventures, from the pee incident to the pink candy debacle. "And I was mean to you when I first met you," I added.

Zoey nodded, smiling. "Keke," she said, "sometimes conditions can be... misunderstood. Santa might take extenuating circumstances into account."

Extenuating circumstances? That sounded hopeful. "So maybe if I'm good between now and Christmas, Santa will consider that and give me presents, anyway?"

"Maybe," she said.

* * *

The next day, I was on my long walk when we encountered Diane, the lady I had stayed with earlier this year when Mommy and Daddy were on vacation.

"Well, hello there," Diane said, picking me up. "And how's my little alpha dog? Did Daddy ever install the sign I suggested to track the number of days you've stayed accident-free?"

I gulped, remembering how I got "confused" between the pee-pee pads and Diane's front door mat.

"No," Daddy answered her. "But she's been pretty good."

I looked at him and wagged my tail.

"Maybe not quite 'nice-list' material yet," Daddy added.

As the two of them chuckled over my fate, Diane must have noticed my drooping ears. "Oh, don't look so worried, Keke." She hugged me closer. "Santa has been known to commute sentences."

I wasn't sure what that meant, but it sounded optimistic. Maybe this was like Wheel of Fortune, where even the losers get some prize money. And there was only a little more than a week left before Christmas. Certainly I could be good between now and then!

I was so happy I could pee, and it was then I remembered Diane was still holding me.

Uh-oh...

Lesson 47: Keke's Christmas Wish

In that day, the wolf and the lamb will live together

Mousey and I played with a fluff ball one morning in the living room. We had less space than usual because the "Christmas tree corner" had grown. Each day this week, Mommy and Daddy added more presents, cutting off more play space and enticing me with questions.

Who were all the gifts for? Would there be any for me, even though I had been bad? Would I make the "nice list"?

The tree towered over me, its long branches decorated with dazzling lights, delicate ornaments, and tinsel. I steered clear of it, careful not to break anything and ruin my history of seven "accident-free" days.

But this morning, the little fluff ball bounced close to the tree, and I trotted after it, not noticing where I was. The ball stopped short of a small wooden building I had not seen before. It was open on three sides and held delicate figurines of a man and a woman with sheep standing nearby. Everyone seemed to look at the baby in the woman's arms.

Mousey interrupted my reverie. "Hey, it's your turn. Hit the ball back."

"What's this?" I asked, indicating the wooden hut.

"I don't know. I think they call it a 'manger.' Hey, that reminds me," Mousey said, excited. "He's coming tonight!"

"Who's coming?" I asked. My tail wagged at the prospect of a visitor.

"Santa!"

"Oh, him. I don't think I'm getting any presents."

"Cheer up!" my friend said. "You heard what the cat said about extenuating circumstances, and you've been really good since then!"

Zoey was the wise old cat who had recently taken up residence in the back room of our house. My best friend, Mousey, was scared of her but reluctantly agreed to enter her lair with me last week to get the inside scoop on Santa's lists.

"I don't know about Christmas," I said. "Something seems kind of 'off' about it."

"What do you mean?"

"Well, take Santa. If I'm good, he's supposed to bring me presents. But what did I get him? It doesn't seem fair."

The question hung in the air like the ornaments on the tree. Just then, a cold wind blew through the house, and I watched the tinsel float momentarily on the breeze. It took a moment to realize someone had entered the front door.

Daddy! I barked as I ran to the door to greet him, and he picked me up and asked, "How's my good girl Keke?"

He called me his good girl!

I wagged my tail and kissed him hello. I looked at the tree in the far corner and the tiny manger resting below. The tree was so large and festive, and the manger so small.

The rest of the day was a whirlwind of activity as delicious smells wafted from the kitchen, visitors came and left, and more boxes appeared beneath the crowded tree. After dark, Mommy and I took our last walk of the evening, and I noticed one of our neighbors had a large manger on their front lawn. Humans, donkeys, and sheep were life-size and illuminated with a bright spotlight. An angel stood in the middle, and in front of him was an empty burlap-lined cot, but the cot was empty.

I slept uneasily that night. I dreamed of the angel and the animals in the outdoor manger. Then suddenly, a bright light shone, and a baby appeared in the cot.

The bright light awoke me, and I realized it was morning.

Mommy got up first. "Merry Christmas, Keke!" she said. "Let's go for a walk, and then we can open presents."

As we walked past our neighbor's house, Mommy said, "Look, Keke. The baby Jesus is in the manger now. It's the Christmas miracle."

I looked at the manger. A statue of a baby lay in the burlap cot, just like in my dream. I wondered where it came from and why it was there.

As if reading my thoughts, Mommy said, "That's baby Jesus, and today is His birthday." And then she told me a story:

"In that day, the wolf and the lamb will live together; the leopard will lie down with the baby goat. The calf and the yearling will be safe with the lion, and a little child will lead them all." -Isaiah 11:6

I didn't see any wolves in the manger, but there were lambs, and I wondered how a little child could lead them.

A little later, we all gathered by the tree to open presents. Mousey was hopping from gift to gift and reading all the tags. "You got one from Santa!" he said. "And so did I! C'mon, open your present!"

As he bit the wrapping on his little present, I said, "Wait! What about Zoey?"

Mousey stopped mid-chew, a tiny piece of paper clinging to the side of his mouth. "What about her?"

"Well, she's part of the family, too. She should be here."

Mousey looked from side to side, whiskers twitching. "B-but what if she steals my present?"

I laughed. "Zoey won't take your present. But it's her Christmas too, and she shouldn't be alone."

Daddy watched me as I walked to the back bedroom. "Where are you off to?" he asked.

When I returned, Zoey trotted beside me, and Daddy raised his eyebrows, looking from dog to cat. "So you two are friends now, eh?" He smiled. "Well, c'mere, Zoey, and join the Christmas party."

Zoey looked around the room, first at Mommy and Daddy, then at Mousey, who was trembling at the sight of the large Tabby approaching. Ignoring the mouse, Zoey jumped on the couch and sat beside Mommy. Her purring grew louder as Mommy rubbed behind her ears.

Hearing the cat's purrs, Mousey relaxed and resumed chewing the paper on his gift.

I savored the wrapping on my present and did not notice Zoey jumping down from the couch and quietly unwrapping her gift.

Neither did Mousey until his present was freed from the paper. It was a small plastic lattice ball with a bell in the middle. The bell jingled as the ball moved, and when Mousey turned to look, he discovered Zoey observing him closely.

"Um, no problem," said the mouse. "You can have it." Trembling, he shoved the ball and watched it roll to the cat, the little bell jingling inside as it moved.

Zoey extended her paw and tapped the ball, which rolled back. The mouse stood transfixed as the ball rolled slowly across the floor and stopped with a tap on his nose.

"It's okay," the cat said. "Just give it a push."

The mouse nudged the ball harder this time, and the cat watched it roll before trapping it with her paw. This time, she rolled it to me. I put my present aside and joined the game, hitting the jingling ball back to Mousey. Mousey giggled and tapped it with her nose, which went off course and rolled toward the little wooden manger under the tree.

"Oh, sorry, sorry!" squeaked the mouse.

"No big deal," assured Zoey, catching the ball.

I watched my friends play. If a wolf and lamb could live together, perhaps a mouse and cat could, too. Was this part of the Christmas miracle?

"I think Jesus wants everyone to play together," I said.

Mommy got on the floor and addressed the woman holding the baby in our manger. "What do you think, Mary? Can you help the rest of the world learn to play together, too? That's all I want for Christmas."

I looked at the smiling mother holding the baby in the manger. As I turned away, I thought I heard someone say, "Peace."

Appendix A: I Got Puppy Scammed and Lived to Write About It

With ten tips to help you avoid being her next victim

It was all Bella's fault.

I know it's irresponsible to blame a scam on a puppy that never existed. But she looked like a 'Bella' in the pictures; we just had to name her. She had that cute Yorkie face and dark features reminiscent of a sweet Italian girl. But it was the facial expression that sold the name. Vulnerable and trusting. She was waiting for us to come and get her.

'Bella' is a name I associate with a young girl. In my eyes, the puppy will always be childlike and dainty, no matter how old she gets—*una bella ragazza*. She will need us to protect her from the evils of the world, the vicious dogs and cats. And yes, unscrupulous humans.

We failed on that last one. Miserably.

We had little experience naming dogs. We'd had only two in the last thirty years. We got them both as puppies and never stopped loving them until they passed from natural causes. Each left a hole when they departed.

Could Bella fill a little of that void? We believed she could.

My wife and I had been looking for a puppy for a few months but hadn't found any local breeders with a small dog like a Teacup Yorkie. We weren't particular about the breed; we just wanted a small dog we could bring when we traveled that friends wouldn't mind watching occasionally. One we could train with love.

There was a pet store within an hour's drive that had numerous breeds, including Yorkies, but one visit raised alarms. They wouldn't even tell us the price of a dog until we went through yards of paperwork establishing our financials and committing to a single dog. And they got their dogs from all over the country, not from local breeders.

We monitored rescue shelters, but they rarely had young puppies. Small breeds were tough to find.

So, we expressed interest when Charlotte Whybird popped up on Facebook with pictures of her Teacup Yorkies about a five-hour drive away, with testimonials (also on Facebook) to her reputation as a breeder and the very reasonable price of $650.

Lesson #1: If it sounds too good to be true, it probably is.

Yorkie puppies usually sell for $2,000-$3,000. We knew this, but we lived on a budget, and $3,000 would require giving up something else. We thought we were being thrifty.

Meanwhile, Charlotte asked questions about us to verify we would give the puppy a good home. It made us trust her.

"The scammer's intention is to establish a relationship as quickly as possible, endear himself to the victim, and gain trust."—U.S. Federal Bureau of Investigation website

She said we could visit the three females in the litter in two weeks and pick one out, but as the days went by, two of the three were spoken for, and someone else wanted the third. If we wanted a puppy from this litter, we'd need to put down a "totally refundable" $250 deposit, and we'd have to do it immediately.

The screenshot below was sent from Charlotte Whybird to show her chat with another customer who supposedly wanted Bella

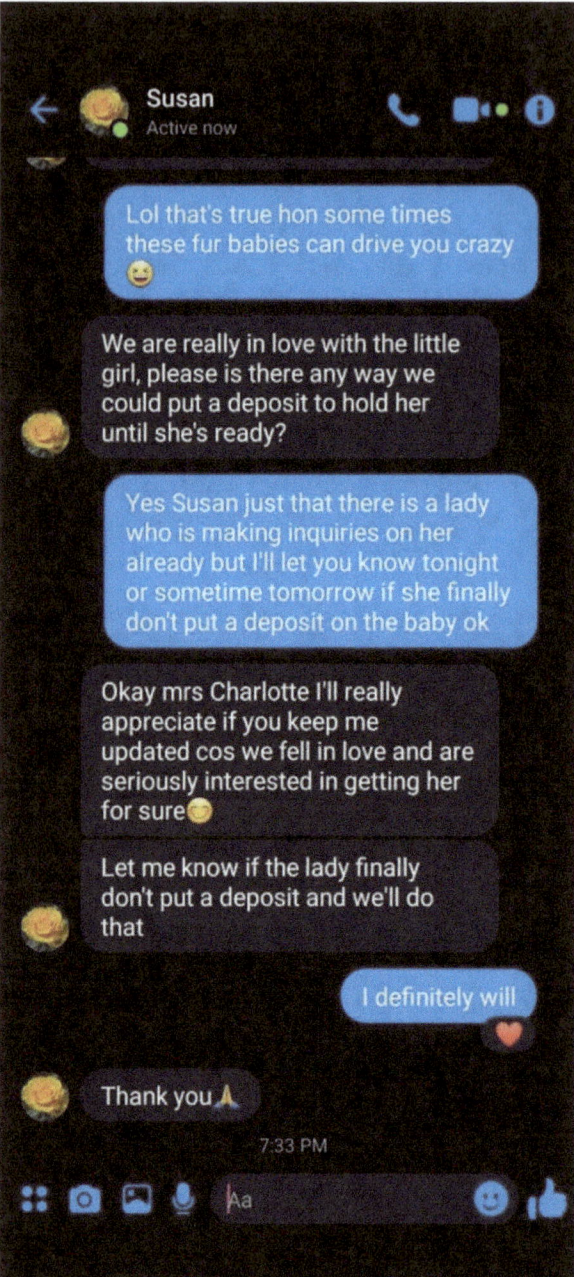

Lesson #2: Scammers want you to act before you have time to think.

Of course, there was the chance the puppies were selling quickly, and we didn't want to miss out on Bella.

Charlotte wouldn't accept PayPal or a credit card, so we set up a Zelle account and rushed a $250 payment.

Lesson #3: Don't pay using cash apps.

"Credit cards (and PayPal) offer legal protections not found with other methods."—*Consumer Reports website*

All the while, Charlotte gave good answers to our questions about puppy care and recommended quality food. We made plans to see Bella in person the following weekend. She told us we could take her home, even though she would only be seven weeks old.

Lesson #4: Stay away from breeders who don't follow proper breeding rules.

Any breeder should know that puppies should not leave their mother before eight weeks. They're either a scammer or an irresponsible breeder if they cut corners on puppy care. Either way, steer clear.

We tried to plan an extra trip to see Bella early, but Charlotte was always unavailable.

Lesson #5: A reputable breeder will allow you to see your puppy in advance.

Finally, it was the day before we planned to drive to the breeder's place, meet Bella, and take her home. We got an urgent text from Charlotte saying her father was very sick, and she had to leave town immediately to visit him. She offered to arrange for the delivery of our puppy at a transport cost of $100. We were in deep now, and Bella was our baby. How could we risk losing her for

$100 extra? So, we rushed off another payment with Zelle.

A couple of hours later, the transport company contacted us and requested $450 for insurance and $150 for a rabies shot.

Lesson #6: Scammers like to work through incremental payments.

Instead of scaring you off with a big-ticket price up-front, they start small, hook you, then add more charges.

The transport company went by a legitimate business name. I looked them up. However, their email address did not match the domain name of the transport they claimed to represent. It was too late in the day to call the company to verify things independently, but I had taken "anti-phishing" training at work and knew that mismatched domain names were a common way for cybercriminals to make it appear they were someone they were not.

Lesson #7: Scammers pretend to be from a legitimate organization, often one you know.

The rabies shot also sparked concern: Bella was too young to have one.

We were heartbroken, but the red flags were piling up. Still unwilling to let go, we gave Charlotte an ultimatum. We would only make further payments once we had Bella in our arms; otherwise, we wanted our money back. We exchanged many more text messages, and our urgent requests to talk by phone went unheeded.

Lesson #8: Scammers prefer to work by text messaging apps.

"The best way to get to know a breeder is to meet in person, which might be at their kennel or in their home. If that's not possible, ask to meet your breeder and their dogs via a video-conferencing system."—American Kennel Club

When we refused to pay the extra fees to the shipper, Charlotte told us she would leave Bella outside that night because we hadn't paid in time for the transport to pick her up. Anything that happened to her was our fault.

Lesson #9: Scammers use emotional blackmail.

Once the mark is personally invested, they become susceptible to many attacks.

Okay, so it wasn't Bella's fault. It was our fault for naming the puppy we'd never seen, giving us a huge emotional attachment, and leaving ourselves open to scams.

We reported Charlotte and the fake transport company to the police (with little hope of seeing any return). We were lucky to get out of the scam with only $350 lost from our checking account. Our emotional bank account, on the other hand, was far more depleted. Bella was gone, and we didn't have the heart to look for another puppy.

Epilogue

Eventually, we thought about puppies again. We researched puppy scams and puppy mills. We put the word out that we were looking for a puppy and eventually found a friend who recommended a local breeder. We learned more about the breeder and visited her in person.

That's how we found an energetic, strong-willed, precocious Biewer Terrier puppy, raised correctly and socialized before we bought her at ten weeks old. Our breeder, Sharon Temple of Yorkies by the Lake in Lake Panasofkee, Florida (https://www.facebook.com/YorkiesbytheLake), was everything a breeder should be. She answered all our questions about her operation, caring for this breed of puppy, and her lineage. We saw the kennel and met the puppy's parents.

When we got her home, we considered naming the puppy 'Bella.' But in truth, Bella was dead, and there could never be another. Besides, she didn't look like a 'Bella.' We finally settled on the name 'Keke.'

My final lesson relates to lesson #9 and helps avoid emotional blackmail:

Lesson #10: Don't name your puppy until the papers are signed, the payments made, and she's home in your arms.

We were a little guarded in letting Keke into our hearts, but she turned out to be just the sweet filling we needed to top up the hole left empty by Bella. We were ready to love a puppy again.

Make your ending happy

There might be a puppy somewhere waiting for you. To learn more about puppy scams, visit reputable websites like The American Kennel Club (https://www.akc.org) and the U.S. Humane Society (https://www.humanesociety.org). Here is an excellent place to start: https://www.akc.org/expert-advice/advice/spot-puppy-scam

Once you've become an educated consumer, go find your puppy. Bella Fortuna!

Conclusion

Thank you! Ratings and reviews are essential for authors because they help others find our books! Please consider posting a review on Amazon or wherever you purchased this book. **Click this link or copy it to your browser to rate this book:**

https://vancamp.info/review-keke-book1

Contact Keke (and Ken):

Keke loves to hear from her fans. Tell us what lessons you liked or didn't care for, to help us improve! You can contact us via email, Facebook, or our blogs on Medium or Substack. Here are some specifics:

Email: kekesguide@gmail.com

Facebook: https://facebook.com/kekesguide

Website: https://www.vancamp.info/

Follow Keke's blog:

On Medium: https://medium.com/kekesguide (Medium membership costs $5/month or $50/year)

On Substack: https://kekesguide.substack.com (FREE)

Follow Keke's podcast:

Search for "Keke's Guide" on your favorite podcast player (FREE) and FOLLOW to be notified whenever new episodes are posted. The Keke's Guide podcast is streaming on all podcast apps.

YES! Keke has merch!!!

You can buy Keke's Guide merchandise at the following online store. Take Keke with you wherever you go!

https://kekes-guide.printify.me/products

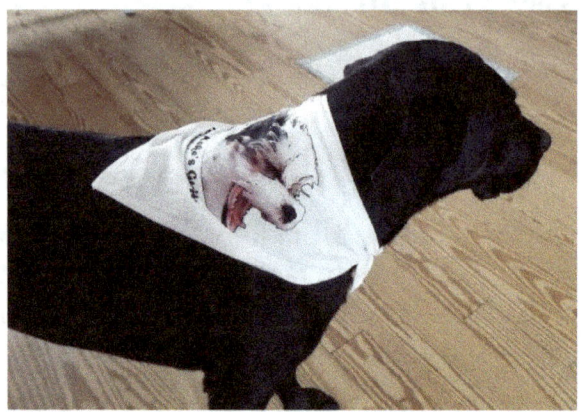

Keke's Guide Pet bandana

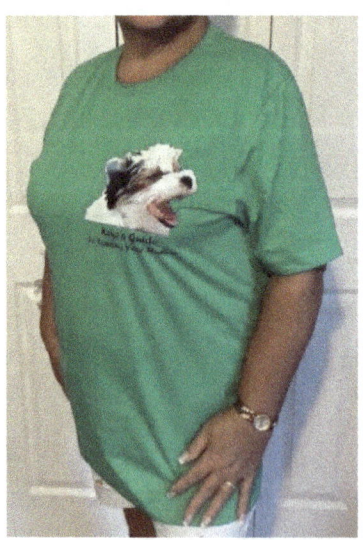

Keke's Guide teeshirt

www.ingramcontent.com/pod-product-compliance
Lightning Source LLC
Chambersburg PA
CBHW070700130626
46553CB00005B/1782